A JOURNEY OF RICHES

The Attitude of Gratitude

12 Stories of Refining the Art of Appreciation

A Journey of Riches – The Attitude of Gratitude

12 Stories of Refining the Art of Appreciation © 2020

Published by Motion Media International
Editing: Gwendolyn Parker, Chris Drabenstott, Daniel Decillis, and Vanessa Corr
Cover Design: Motion Media International
Typesetting & Assembly: Motion Media International
Printing: Amazon and Ingram Sparks

Creator: John Spender - Primary Author
Title: *A Journey Of Riches - The Attitude of Gratitude*
ISBN Digital: 978-1-925919-23-3
ISBN Print: 978-1-925919-26-4
Subjects: Self-Help, Motivation/Inspiration and Spirituality.

Acknowledgments

R eading and writing is a gift that very few give to themselves. It is such a powerful way to reflect and gain closure from the past; reading and writing is a therapeutic process. The experience raises one's self-esteem, confidence, and awareness of self.

I learned this when I collated the first book in the *A Journey of Riches* series, which now includes twenty-two books with over 250 different co-authors from more than forty different countries. It's not easy to write about your personal experiences, and I honor and respect every one of the authors who have collaborated in the series thus far.

For many of the authors, English is their second language, which is a significant achievement in itself. In creating this anthology of short stories, I have been touched by the amount of generosity, gratitude, and shared energy that this experience has given everyone.

The inspiration for *A Journey of Riches, The Attitude of Gratitude* was a suggestion from Joanne Singleton who reached out to me in April 2020 suggesting we relate the theme for the next book in the *A Journey of Riches* series to fit in with the global pandemic. The first sub title was *Gratefulness in the Midst of a Pandemic* I later change it to *The Attitude of Gratitude* as I felt this theme will stand the test of time and be a fan favorite for our growing readership. You can never go wrong with a grateful heart.

Naturally, I could not have created this book without the eleven other co-authors who all said "YES" when I asked them to share their insights and wisdom. Just as each chapter in this book makes for inspiring reading, each story represents one chapter in the life of each of the authors, with the chief aim of having you, the reader, live a more inspired life. Together we can embrace gratitude and all the miracles that this attitude brings to ones life.

I want to thank all the authors for entrusting me with their unique memories, encounters, and wisdom. Thank you for sharing and opening the door to your soul so that others may learn from your experience. I trust the readers will gain confidence from your successes, and also the wisdom you gained from your failures.

I also want to thank my family. I know you are proud of me, seeing how far I have come from that 10-year-old boy who was learning how to read and write at a basic level. Big shout out to my Mom, Robert, Dad, and Merril; my brother, Adam, and his daughter, Krystal; my sister, Hollie, her partner, Brian, my nephew Charlie, and niece, Heidi—thank you for your support. Also, kudos to my grandparents: Gran and Pop, who are alive and well, and Ma and Pa, who now rest in peace. They accept me just the way I am with all my travels and adventures around the world.

Thanks to all the team at Motion Media International; you have done an excellent job at editing and collating this book. It was a pleasure working with you on this successful project, and I thank you for your patience in dealing with the various changes and adjustments along the way.

Thank you, the reader, for having the courage to look at your life and how you can improve your future in a fast and rapidly changing world.

Thank you again to my fellow co-authors: Simone Waddell, Tina Louise Vercillo, Patrick Oei, Jacinta Legg, Elizabeth Ross-Boag, Julie Blouin, King Gabriel Quincy Collymore, Kyle de Mole, Joanne Singleton, Monique Sayers and Anup Batra.

We would greatly appreciate an honest review on Amazon if this book inspires you. This is how we gain more readers to our inspiring book!

With gratitude,
John Spender

Praise for *A Journey of Riches* Book Series

"The *A Journey of Riches* book series is a great collection of inspiring short stories that will leave you wanting more!"

~ Alex Hoffmann, Network Marketing Guru.

"If you are looking for an inspiring read to get you through any change, this is it!! This book is comprised of many gripping perspectives from a collection of successful international authors with a tone of wisdom to share."

~ Theera Phetmalaigul, Entrepreneur/Investor.

"*A Journey of Riches* is an empowering series that implements two simple words in overcoming life's struggles.

By diving into the meaning of the words "problem" and "challenge," you will find yourself motivated to believe in the triumph of perseverance. With many different authors from all around the world coming together to share various stories of life's trials, you will find yourself drenched in encouragement to push through even the darkest of battles.

The stories are heartfelt personal shares of moving through and transforming challenges into rich life experiences.

The book will move, touch and inspire your spirit to face and overcome any of life's adversities. It is a truly inspirational read. Thank you for being the kind open soul you are, John!!"

~ Casey Plouffe, Seven Figure Network Marketer.

"A must-read for anyone facing major changes or challenges in life right now. This book will give you the courage to move through any struggle with confidence, grace, and ease."

~ Jo-Anne Irwin, Transformational Coach
and Best-selling Author.

"I have enjoyed the *Journey of Riches* book series. Each person's story is written from the heart, and everyone's journey is different. We all have a story to tell, and John Spender does an amazing job of finding authors, and combining their stories into uplifting books."

~ Liz Misner Palmer, Foreign Service Officer.

"A timely read as I'm facing a few challenges right now. I like the various insights from the different authors. This book will inspire you to move through any challenge or change that you are experiencing."

~ David Ostrand, Business Owner.

"I've known John Spender for a while now, and I was blessed with an opportunity to be in book four in the series. I know that you will enjoy this new journey like the rest of the books in the series. The collection of stories will assist you with making changes, dealing with challenges, and seeing that transformation is possible for your life."

~ Charlie O' Shea, Entrepreneur.

"*A Journey of Riches* series will draw you in and help you dig deep into your soul. Authors have unbelievable life stories of purpose inside of them. John Spender is dedicated to bringing peace, love, and adventure to the world of his readers! Dive into this series, and you will be transformed!"

~ Jeana Matichak, Author of *Finding Peace*.

"Awesome! Truly inspirational! It is amazing what the human spirit can achieve and overcome! Highly recommended!!"

~ Fabrice Beliard, Australian Business Coach
and Best-selling Author.

"*A Journey of Riches* Series is a must-read. It is an empowering collection of inspirational and moving stories full of courage, strength, and heart. Bringing peace and awareness to those lucky enough to read to assist and inspire them on their life journey."

~ Gemma Castiglia, Avalon Healing and Best-selling Author.

"The *A Journey of Riches* book series is an inspirational collection of books that will empower you to take on any challenge or change in life."

~ Kay Newton, Midlife Stress Buster
and Best-selling Author.

"*A Journey of Riches* book series is an inspiring collection of stories, sharing many different ideas and perspectives on how to overcome challenges, deal with change and to make empowering choices in your life. Open the book anywhere and let your mood choose where you need to read. Buy one of the books today; you'll be glad that you did!"

~ Trish Rock, Modern Day Intuitive,
Best-selling Author, Speaker, Psychic, and Holistic Coach.

"*A Journey of Riches* is another inspiring read. The authors are from all over the world, and each has a unique perspective to share, that will have you thinking differently about your current circumstances in life. An insightful read!"

~ Alexandria Calamel, Success Coach and Best-selling Author.

"The *A Journey of Riches* book series is a collection of real-life stories, which are truly inspiring and give you the confidence that no matter what you are dealing with in your life, there is a light at the end of the tunnel, and a very bright one at that. Totally empowering!"

~ John Abbott, Freedom Entrepreneur.

"An amazing collection of true stories from individuals who have overcome great changes and who have transformed their lives and used their experience to uplift, inspire and support others."

~ Carol Williams, Author-Speaker-Coach.

"You can empower yourself from the power within this book that can help awaken the sleeping giant within you. John has a purpose in life to bring inspiring people together to share their wisdom for the benefit of all who venture deep into this book series. If you are looking for inspiration to be someone special, this book can be your guide."

~ Bill Bilwani, Renowned Melbourne Restaurateur.

"In the *A Journey Of Riches* series, you will catch the impulse to step up, reconsider and settle for only the very best for yourself and those around you. Penned from the heart and with an unflinching drive to make a difference for the good of all, *A Journey Of Riches* series is a must-read."

~ Steve Coleman, Author of *Decisions, Decisions! How to Make the Right One Every Time.*

"Do you want to be on top of your game? *A Journey of Riches* is a must-read with breakthrough insights that will help you do just that!"

~ Christopher Chen, Entrepreneur.

"In *A Journey of Riches*, you will find the insight, resources, and tools you need to transform your life. By reading the author's stories, you, too, can be inspired to achieve your greatest accomplishments and what is truly possible for you. Reading this book activates your true potential for transforming your life way beyond what you think is possible. Read it and learn how you, too, can have a magical life."

~ Elaine Mc Guinness,
Best-selling Author of *Unleash Your Authentic Self!*

"If you are looking for an inspiring read, look no further than the *A Journey of Riches* book series. The books are an inspiring collection of short stories that will encourage you to embrace life even more. I highly recommend you read one of the books today!"

~ Kara Dono, Doula, Healer and Best-selling Author.

"*A Journey of Riches* series is a must-read for anyone seeking to enrich their own lives and gain wisdom through the wonderful stories of personal empowerment & triumphs over life's challenges. I've given several copies to my family, friends, and clients to inspire and support them to step into their greatness. I highly recommend that you read these books, savoring the many 'aha's' and tools you will discover inside."

~ Michele Cempaka, Hypnotherapist, Shaman, Transformational Coach, and Reiki Master.

"If you are looking for an inspirational read, look no further than the *A Journey of Riches* book series. The books are an inspiring and educational collection of short stories from the author's soul that will encourage you to embrace life even more. I've even given them to my clients too so that their journeys inspire them in life for wealth, health and everything else in between. I recommend you make it a priority to read one of the books today!"

~ Goro Gupta, Chief Education Officer, Mortgage Terminator, and Property Mentor.

"The *A Journey of Riches* book series is filled with real-life short stories of heartfelt tribulations turned into uplifting, self-transformation by the power of the human spirit to overcome adversity. The journeys captured in these books will encourage you to embrace life in a whole new way. I highly recommend reading this inspiring anthology series."

~ Chris Drabenstott, Best-selling Author, and Editor.

"There is so much motivational power in the *A Journey of Riches* series!! Each book is a compilation of inspiring, real-life stories by several different authors, which makes the journey feel more relatable and success more attainable. If you are looking for something to move you forward, you'll find it in one (or all) of these books."

~ Cary MacArthur, Personal Empowerment Coach

"I've been fortunate to write with John Spender and now, I call him a friend. *A Journey of Riches* book series features real stories that have inspired me and will inspire you. John has a passion for finding amazing people from all over the world, giving the series a global perspective on relevant subject matters."

~ Mike Campbell, Fat Guy Diary, LLC

"The *A Journey of Riches* series is the reflection of beautiful souls who have discovered the fire within. Each story takes you inside the truth of what truly matters in life. While reading these stories, my heart space expanded to understand that our most significant contribution in this lifetime is to give and receive love. May you also feel inspired as you read this book."

~ Katie Neubaum, Author of *Transformation Calling*.

"*A Journey of Riches* is an inspiring testament that love and gratitude are the secret ingredients to living a happy and fulfilling life. This series is sure to inspire and bless your life in a big way. Truly an inspirational read that is written and created by real people, sharing real-life stories about the power and courage of the human spirit."

~ Jen Valadez, Emotional Intuitive and Best-selling Author

Table of Contents

Preface

I collated this book and chose the various authors to share their experiences about how they have developed the attitude of gratitude in their life. The eclectic collection of chapters encompasses a myriad of different writing styles and perspectives that demonstrate what is possible when we recognise and appreciate the good that is present in our life.

Like all of us, each author has a unique story and insight to share with you. It might so happen that one or more authors have lived through an experience similar to circumstances in your life. Their words could be just the words you need to read to help you through your challenges and motivate you to continue on your chosen path.

Storytelling has been the way humankind has communicated ideas and learning throughout our civilization. While we have become more sophisticated with technology, and living in the modern world is more convenient, there is still much discontent and dissatisfaction. Many people have also moved away from reading books, and they are missing valuable information that can help them move forward in life with a positive outlook. Moving towards the tasks or dreams that scare us breeds confidence growing towards becoming better versions of ourselves.

I think it is essential to turn off the TV—to slow down and to read, reflect, and take the time to appreciate everything you have in life. Start with an anthology book as they offer a cornucopia of viewpoints relating to a particular theme. In this case, it's fear and how others have dealt with it. I think the reason why we feel stuck in life or have challenges in a particular area is that we see the problem through the same lens that created it. With this compendium and all of the books in the *A Journey of Riches* series, you have many different writing styles and perspectives that will help you think and see your challenges differently, motivating you to elevate your set of circumstances.

Anthology books are also great because you can start from any chapter and gain valuable insight or a nugget of wisdom without the feeling that you have missed something from the earlier episodes.

I love reading many different types of personal development books because learning and personal growth are vital. If you are not learning and growing, well, you're staying the same. Everything in the universe is growing, expanding, and changing. If we are not open to different ideas and a multitude of ways to think and be, then even the most skilled and educated among us can become close-minded.

The concept of this book series is to open you up to diverse ways of perceiving your reality. It is to encourage you and give you many avenues of thinking about the same subject. My wish for you is to feel empowered to make a decision that will best suit you in moving forward with your life. As Albert Einstein said, **"We cannot solve problems with the same level of thinking that created them."** With Einstein's words in mind, let your mood pick a chapter in the book, or read from the beginning to the end and be guided to find the answers you seek.

If you feel inspired, we would love an honest review on Amazon. This will help create awareness around this fantastic series of books.

With gratitude,
John Spender

"Gratitude will shift you to a higher frequency, and you will attract much better things."

~ Rhonda Byrne

CHAPTER ONE

The Power of Praise

By John Spender

It was an embarrassing moment when Mrs. Pearce pulled me aside at my high school canteen and, in a stern, commanding voice, reprimanded me for asking the other kids in the canteen line for their change. She called it begging. I delivered her local newspaper, so Mrs. Pearce knew I was earning money. She didn't know that my mom was keeping that money for our family's first "real" summer vacation to the Gold Coast later that year. Back in the early 90s, I was making between $8-14 per day from asking my fellow students for money and about $20 from our family paper run, walking the streets rolling newspapers and placing them in the letterbox at the crack of dawn.

Judgment aside, I know which of the two income-generating activities I enjoyed more and why. One of the reason's I was so successful at begging was that I poured love into my spiel. I looked them directly in the eye with a big smile, offering words of praise for their appearance or a character trait that most people didn't notice. Through praising my peers, I had bulging pockets full of gold and silver coins. Ever since I can remember, I have enjoyed speaking uplifting words into people; I didn't quite have the level of consciousness to fully comprehend the power of genuine praise.

Growing up wearing secondhand clothes or the cheapest clothes from Best n Less or Kmart, my mom taught me how to stretch a dollar, that's for sure. I had the most affordable school shorts you could buy. They were called stubby ruggers and they looked terrible. Most of my friends wore corduroy shorts, even those who lived in the housing commission (cheap housing provided by the government). I never complained to my mom, as I knew how hard she worked to provide for my two siblings and me. We always had enough food and it was healthy food, but at times, I craved a packet of chips or a meat pie. I decided to ask the other kids for their change as they left the canteen with the idea of buying some chunk food. All I had was a charming personality and uplifting energy to pour into them.

At the time, I didn't see the teacher's problem with my actions; I thought I was being resourceful while praising others and myself. After five days, I had enough money to buy two pairs of corduroy shorts because they were on sale. I also had change left over to purchase new tropical fish for my secondhand aquarium that my mother had bought for my birthday earlier that year. Badda bing badda boom…not bad for a 15-year-old rebel!

Life is a state of consciousness; whatever you put out will be reflected back to you. The world around you is a reflection of the state of your mindset as you see life. Your beliefs will be reflected back to you through your experiences. Who you are is another way of expressing the quantum truth of consciousness? We see not *as it is but as we are in our beingness* in any given moment. Once you understand this, the relation between consciousness and gratitude or a state of praise is easy to see. We elevate our consciousness by seeking the expansion of our appreciation for everything that comes our way. Switching to a "heartset" of kindness towards all life increases through our benevolent deeds—praise the good we see, and we will have heaven on earth. Praise consciousness is like a mustard seed that grows and expands until it becomes the greatest of herbs. To expand a balloon, you fill it with air. To expand water, you apply heat. To expand a seed, you bury it in soil. To expand gratitude, you offer praise. The consciousness of praise is something we must learn to cultivate, nurture, and grow.

Croft M. Pentz, one of the greatest clergymen of our time, said, "Praise, like sunlight, helps all things to grow." All of creation responds to praise. Animal trainers pet and reward their animals with treats for acts of obedience. Children glow with happiness when they are praised. Even vegetation grows better for those who provide love and care. When we speak words of encouragement and appreciation to our own abilities, our brain cells augment and increase in capacity and intelligence. Praise and gratitude create the same vibration and frequency of positivity and are like inseparable identical twins; where you find one, you'll find the other. Giving praise is expressing your appreciation, which creates an attitude and environment that is magnetic to other people. Giving praise heals disease, removes obstacles, and it will even open prison doors in the mind; it will do things for us that we can't do for ourselves.

The quickest way to connect and form a communion with the substance of supply is through giving praise. Fat Boy Slim was on to something with his worldwide hit dance track "Praise You" with the lyrics:

> *We've come a long, long way together*
> *Through the hard times and the good*
> *I have to celebrate you, baby*
> *I have to praise you like I should.*

When a DJ plays this song, you can feel the good vibes increase on the dance floor in an instant. What is the central object of your praise? What is it that you value the most? Is it your family? Well, praise them. Is it your wife? Praise her. Whatever you value, make praise the foundation and the very presence of your being. Was your breakfast good? Say so; speak it out loud. Did you have a good day at the office? Then, express it. Ride the wave of gratitude; acknowledge your blessings and watch them multiply.

Looking out the window as I take a break from writing, I stare at a large mango tree, obviously suffering from its shabby-looking leaves, probably due to a lack of water, nutrients, and maybe even severed roots from the newly-built home. When I saw that tree, I imagined it was healthy with new shoots of green sprouting out all over its canopy. I would send it positive thoughts praising the tree for the shade it provided, the shelter for birds, and the delicious fruits that it was sure to bear. Some may say this is wacky or even kooky for me. I guess it was a combination of my love for nature and the influence of Dr. David R. Hawkins and his book *Power vs. Force*. In a nutshell, the book is a scientific manifesto of how to use the power we have within our own consciousness as a scale of frequency.

Dr. Hawkins demonstrated through a series of tests in front of live audiences around the world that the subconscious is a living organism that is attuned to recognizing the difference between negative or positive effects on the body. The test required you to place your fingers on someone's arm and push down. When the person is thinking positive thoughts, you won't be able to push their arm down. When the subject thinks negative thoughts, the arm is easily pushed downwards. You begin by pushing their arm down with your fingers. This is easy to test with a friend, and it's a tool that I use in my trainings.

Moreover, when I began to understand Dr. Hawkins' scale of consciousness and the frequency that different emotional states emit, I started experimenting with that Mango tree. I was astounded to see, after a week of sending positive vibes in the way of mental appreciation and praise, the tree began shooting new leaves, and a couple of weeks later, my neighbor began watering his garden. I encourage you create your own experiment putting praise to the test, or at the very least, try Dr. Hawkins' kinesiology process.

Praise the universe for what you have, and you will receive more of it. Praise her in advance for what you do not have, and those things will be attracted to you through your gratitude and expectation. Bless your business, your employees, your customers, and your bank balance; bless every form of good that you receive. If you want a better job, bless the position you are in. If you are unemployed, bless the perfect position that's waiting for you. With thanksgiving, let your request be known to the universe. Thank the Divine for all the good you wish to receive with an underlying knowingness, and good will be provided in return. Bless your home, your family, your neighbors, your friends, your pets; let the invisible force of praise bless your life. The quickest way to happiness is through the power of praise. Give thanks to everything that happens to you, even in crisis, for it is certain that when you express appreciation for it, you transform unfortunate circumstances into a blessing that becomes a valuable lesson and a gift that will serve you for a lifetime.

How will you amplify your consciousness for gratitude except by praising all that you have? Review this chapter up until this point and you will see that I have emphasized four main points:

1. The significance of changing your consciousness

2. The significance of keeping your creator in the forefront of your consciousness

3. The significance of expanding your consciousness

4. The significance of giving praise

This chapter is really a study of consciousness and developing an understanding of its expansion. Grasping this is of vital importance, as consciousness is the medium through which everything enters or leaves your life. Meditation changes things because it expands your consciousness; it aligns you with your purpose, enabling you to accept and see yourself with an atmosphere of gratitude. Meditation naturally attracts this beingness into your external reality. Consciousness reaches its highest level through the self-forgetfulness that meditation brings to your life. Science has now caught up with what metaphysics has been teaching for years. The science of meditation indicates changes in brain wave frequency expanding one's level of awareness and, in turn, growing your consciousness.

The trouble with most people who find themselves down and unable to feel grateful for anything is the obsession they have with themselves. They do not realize that their lack of gratitude is the very thing that defeats them and holds them in want, lack, and desperation. What do we say to these people? We shall tell them that the outcome of their difficulty depends entirely on their attitude and habits of mind. If the mind can be kept at least 51%

positive at such a time, your attitude will shift into ascending amounts of good vibes; liberation is assured. The attitude or habits of the mind are the determining factors in every problem. Additionally, in determining how the faculties of the mind will work, one's attitude shapes the speed in which the consciousness will be elevated. Attitude is the cornerstone to raising one's awareness beyond the self. If one's mental level is kept above the 50% positive over negative, the mind will work with the concept of praise to open the door to the successful and abundant side of life. If it falls below 50% positive, it will act with failure and lack, accentuating and attracting the difficulties in life. How shall we increase the mental level in a global pandemic? By changing our attitude and expecting the best from every person, place, and thing. Ralph Waldo Emerson wrote, "Assume a virtue if you have it not." That is good advice, and we can begin now by assuming our desired virtues through meditation from the circumference to the hub. The circumference represents negative aspects of oneself and the hub is our center, the home of our highest virtuous self, and the door always opens inwards from our outer reality to our inner reality. A grateful heart can and will develop swiftly once you embrace meditation and all its forms into your daily life. I'll expand on this in the next paragraph.

The first step in expanding your praise consciousness is to make meditation the central point of focus. This action will give the mind an upward and forward look, gifting you with a raise in consciousness. The next step is to reverse every negative thought the instant it appears by giving all your power to the consciousness of good. Give no power to failure, delay, doubt, disappointment, despondency, despair, misfortune, or bad luck. Don't get upset when things don't go as expected, and don't expect the worst. Know that your mind has the power to make anything right. Refuse to remain depressed, disappointed, worried, hesitant, or fearful of uncertainty. When trouble and misfortune come your way, remember that they are only temporary. If you are compelled to raise your degree of consciousness, make sure you are doing some form of meditation, be it traditional meditation, walking in nature, staring at the deep blue ocean, gazing at a fiery sunset, or even quieting your mind as you do the dishes.

Do not let interruptions, recessions, or even global pandemics cause you to lose focus of your highest good. When you meet conflict or disharmony, refuse to become divided or distressed in your thoughts. Remember not to get upset with people or situations; both are powerless without your reaction. Hold rigid to the statement of the Dalai Lama: "When you lose, don't lose the lesson." Look upon defeat, failure, and mistakes as moldable plasticine in your hand. Maintain the attitude and feeling of gratitude that will awaken and bring out the best that's inside of you. Know that you can change your circumstances and state of affairs by changing your consciousness through the power of meditation. It makes no difference how poorly things may be going in the outer world; your job is to keep things running smoothly in your own heart and mind. The more you become conscious of your mind, the more your superconscious power will produce results for you. That is the law of attraction. If you train your mind to think in terms of praise, appreciation, and abundance, you will experience an increase in every area of your life. When you give thanks, you continue to receive more things to be thankful for in abundant measure.

Commit now to daily meditation. Begin with five minutes a day, then gradually increase the duration of time. Find a quiet place and sit in comfort. Allow yourself to be still and rest within, focusing on your breath. If you become distracted (and you will!), simply observe the thoughts, then bring your focus back to your breath. Gradually, through repetition and consistency of practice, you will "lose the mind," awakening your senses to the magnificence of your inner world. Slowly but surely, your consciousness will ascend to another level of awareness, embodying higher frequencies and mental states such as gratitude, appreciation, thankfulness, heightened sensitivity, and an energized beingness. In this enlightened state of embodiment, praise comes naturally.

"Every condition, every experience in life is a result of our mental attitude. We can do only what we think and feel we can do. We can be only what we think we can be. We can have only what we think we can have. What we do, who we are, and what we have all depend upon what we think. There is only one limit upon the Creative Force, and that is the limit we impose upon it." These were wise words from one of the greatest self-help authors of the 20th century, Robert Collier. All things are possible when we increase our level of consciousness. We can never express anything that we don't have an awareness of in our field of perception. The secret of all power and all success is found through the cognizance of your consciousness. Allow your meditation practice to guide you into an ever-deeper expansion of your consciousness. Watch as your natural attitude evolves towards praise and appreciation for everything in your world.

Eleven Key Principles to Align with Praise and Gratitude

Allow the following principles to guide and elevate you to the consciousness highway of goodness, grace, and gratitude:

1. Trust in and surrender to the intelligence that created you. This trust is the foundation for your freedom of expression, which allows you to choose how you feel and not be governed by outside circumstances. When you trust yourself, you are no longer afraid to praise another. Higher consciousness is not just an idea that sounds esoteric and spiritual—it's a beingness. Trust is the gateway to developing your higher self. The more you trust the wisdom that creates, the more you'll be trusting in yourself. With trust, you enter the higher realms of frequency, vibration, and consciousness, where expressing gratitude is a natural form of being. In order to unlock gratitude, trust is the first key principle that you must come

to understand and embrace for the embodiment of the other principles.

2. Develop an inner knowing through a deeper, more profound connection with yourself and the universe at large. This discovery of knowing that you are in everything breeds immeasurable connection and appreciation for all things. Embrace your oneness with the universe and know that you are the universe and the universe is you. See the beauty in the unfolding of everyday life. Look for the Divine in the seemingly mundane. Allow your intuition to write the script for your life; let it be the guiding light for your masterpiece. Remember, the intuition is your point of connection, with the universe your creator, and your compass for your greater good. This second principle guides us towards a binding alignment with all things encompassing your higher self.

3. Let go of the lies and smile! It's a lie to think that you aren't good enough. It's a lie to think that you don't deserve to be happy. It's a lie to think that you are not worthy. When you catch yourself thinking one of these erroneous thoughts, just smile. Entwine this counterintuitive principal into your consciousness; smile because, in your heart, you know you are blessed. Smiling to correct an error in your thinking is a form of self-praise. When you let go of the lies, you honor and praise yourself, which creates space for you to praise others. When you can integrate this principle, you will know gratitude.

4. Acknowledge and praise everything that appears in your life, from the Divine to the turbulent, and even the disastrous, for they are leading you towards the greater good in your life. By going within, you will discover that whatever you had experienced bestowed an underlying gift of inner fortitude to overcome anything in your life, or at least to live in harmony with it. When you can look back

with forgiveness and appreciation, even for behavior that doesn't make you proud, you can realize that was who you were at that time and your behaviors had great lessons attached for you to transcend. You will be able to say with certainty, "I am what I am, and the past doesn't reflect my future." While some of the people close to you may find it difficult to accept you, you will no longer compromise yourself. Thanking your past breaks its bondage, creating freedom of choice for this present moment. When you apply this principle, you have made the decision to be free.

5. Align your point of focus. You can't feel praise-worthy and undeserving at the same time. When you catch yourself thinking negative thoughts or about things you don't want, give thanks and bring your attention back to your desires. The law of focus is in operation regardless of whether you are aware of its existence. What you focus on expands, what you focus on seems real, what you focus on you become, so when you focus on the good in your life, the good just gets better. You begin to generate a momentum of goodness that accentuates your sense of gratitude. Aligning your point of focus and employing this principal for your life affirms what is valuable and necessary for your happiness.

6. Be thankful for your good in advance. Perhaps you are suffering through ill health and the prognosis doesn't look good. Give thanks for the good health that is to come. When you look in the mirror, praise yourself as you imagine how good you feel. Doing this is watering the seed of good health that you have planted. In your finances, maybe you are struggling, and business is slow. Affirm with appreciation that whatever you touch prospers and succeeds. Declare your ideal reality throughout the day. When you give thanks in advance, it not only waters your seed, it strengthens your belief and self-esteem. You are praising your ideal life and calibrating yourself with the infinite intelligence of the source of all creation. This

principle will support you to move mountains, making the seemingly impossible possible.

7. Adopt the potency of prayer as a heartfelt form of appreciation for all that is and all that ever will be. Prayer is not just a form of asking, it's also a form of giving praise to your higher self. It's a way to acknowledge yourself and connect deeper within beyond the surface reality of day-to-day living. Develop a sacredness that guides you through prayer. Allow prayer to cultivate the good and rid yourself of ego-dominating thoughts so you can grow your connection to Divinity. Heaven on earth is a choice that we decide to make, not a place we must find.

"Dear Universe/God, I praise you for granting me the inner peace, wisdom, and stability to inspire heaven in my home and community. I thank you for all that I have and all that I am. I appreciate your light that steers me to grow and evolve into the best version of myself, in good health and percipience. And so, it is."

Your dedication to this principle of prayer will open opportunities in your life that you never knew existed.

8. Acknowledge and appreciate the challenges of your lineage. Your ancestors endured struggles and difficulties that paved the way for a better life for you. Maybe they had to cross oceans with the threat of pirates or endure a world war. Be thankful for the struggles and adversity that they undoubtedly conquered just so you can live your life today. Consider visiting the grave site of your ancestors and acknowledge their existence with your presence, praising their lives. Even visiting your local cemetery and praising the lives of another human being's journey will breed the attitude of gratitude within your consciousness. This principle of remembering the evolution of life calls for us to remember those who laid the path for us to walk on.

9. Wake up to the gift of breath. Becoming conscious of your breath is to bring your beingness into present-moment awareness of the here and now, the domain of infinite possibilities. Open up to its tranquil guidance like the touch of the first rays of sunlight of a cool spring morning. Surrender to its softness and unwavering support. Nothing is possible without the breath, yet it is so easy to take it for granted. We can last a month or even longer without food. Without water, we will perish within three to four days. However, the cells in the brain will begin dying within three minutes without oxygen. Spiritual teacher Cristen Rodgers articulates it this way: "Each breath is like a little rebirth, a renaissance that can only be celebrated if we recognise that it's happening." This principle is urging us to heighten our relationship with the breath and recognize its presence with your appreciation.

10. Demonstrate your appreciation and praise for your body temple and the environment at large. When we make venerable choices for our bodies, we align ourselves with the greater good of all. If we can appreciate ourselves, we can praise our planet by adjusting the way we treat it. We have a symbiotic relationship with our environment; what affects one effects the other. A perfect example of this is the sea anemone and the clownfish. They coexist in harmony, each providing a benefit for the other. The anemone provides shelter and protection for the clownfish. In return, the clownfish cleans the anemone from parasites. Their relationship is one of praise. This principle brings us to a place of honoring our symbiotic relationship with the earth through praising our own existence.

11. Declare your gratitude and praise through affirmations. Our brains are not naturally wired for gratitude. Survival is the chief aim of the mind, and without heedful awareness, the mind can automatically run things. To avoid fearful living, repeat positive affirmations to remind and program your mind, expanding your consciousness and heartfelt

gratefulness. Meditating before you affirm anything quiets the mind, shifting the brain from a beta wave frequency to an alpha state. It's a mistake to say your affirmations while not in a positive frame of mind. It's the easiest thing in the world to get caught up with distractions, negativity, and other people's drama and forget about your own dreams and desires. Make this conditioning principle part of your daily ritual meditation to affirm the reality you want to live.

Here are 11 positive affirmations to begin your practice:

* I appreciate all that I am and all that I have.

* I give generously to myself.

* I know what I love to do, and I do it.

* Miracles are love in action.

* Every gift I give serves and empowers others.

* I send love to my fears, which are places within me that await my love.

* Every gift I give is a gift for myself. As I give, I receive.

* As I live in present moment awareness, I live the magic of synchronicity.

* I appreciate myself. I give thanks for my awesome life.

* The things that I create are even better than I imagined them to be.

* I am what I am, and what I am is a spark of God force and that God force is all compassion and forgiveness.

As you embody the above principles, notice how you can evoke overwhelming states of appreciation and practically lose the ability to worry. As you awaken to praise consciousness, accepting your life for all it is and isn't, you'll begin to have frequent, overwhelming episodes of gratitude. Everything becomes a miracle. You become aware of how much you have to praise and appreciate, and there is no room for scantiness or meagerness, as it is no longer your point of focus. With an expanded consciousness of praise, life is no longer a competition but an enrichment of collaboration where everyone wins. You are now living the attitude of gratitude. You over-expand like a balloon and pop into conspicuous levels of consciousness.

"Gratitude is the direct way out of comparison."

~ Robyn Conley Downs

CHAPTER TWO

Healing after Loss:
How Gratitude can Assist in
Coping with Grief

By Julie Blouin

When you start viewing through the lens of gratitude, your mindset shifts immediately. You can turn sadness into happiness and despair into hope.

➢ What if we let go, just for an instant, of the idea that the healing process of grieving the loss of a loved one takes a long time?

➢ What if healing grief is a personal journey without a specific time frame?

➢ What if we stepped away from the five stages of grief most therapists use, which is through these emotions: denial, anger, bargaining, depression, and acceptance?

➢ What if there is an easier way to shift the profound sadness into happiness, despair into hope?

➢ What if there is a formula everyone could understand, from children to seniors?

➢ What if our mindset is the key component to living a happier life and coping with losing a loved one?

Robert A. Emmons, psychologist and professor at the University of California, Davis, who has conducted extensive scientific research on gratitude, states in his book *Gratitude Works!* that: "People who experience gratitude can cope more effectively with everyday stress, show increased resilience in the face of trauma-induced stress, recover more quickly from illness, and enjoy more robust physical health." (P.9-10)

To add to all the research on the effectiveness of gratitude, in this chapter I will explain my own personal journey of grieving over the devastating loss of both my brother when I was only 16 years old, and my mother six years later, through the attitude of gratitude. This chapter will highlight the importance of gratitude and how it can change your life, and I will show you how to integrate gratitude into your everyday life, even if you are not necessarily grieving. My goal is to offer a different perspective on coping with the loss of a loved one. I will keep it simple, and I will clearly explain the coping mechanisms which have helped me heal my profound sadness.

If you are grieving, or if you know someone who recently experienced the loss of a loved one, this is an excellent chapter to read. It will also be useful if you are a mindset coach, a therapist, a life coach, a grief support counselor, a psychologist, a volunteer in palliative care, or anyone working with families through end-of-life assistance. The information here is something I wish I had over two decades ago.

Taking the time to grieve is important, but it is equally important to nourish your mind, body, and soul at the same time. I invite you to navigate through this chapter with an open mind. Let the words sink into your heart and soul. Let's begin.

My grieving journey began on May 19, 1994, just after midnight, when I found out my brother Frederic had passed away in his sleep from heart failure. An overwhelming wave of sadness paralyzed my body. I was completely devastated and heartbroken. How can such a tragedy happen at such a young age?

As I closed my eyes and tried to fall asleep, images kept flashing in my mind, like the scar he had on his chest and abdomen from the open heart surgery he had when he was only a toddler, and how his lips would sometimes turn blue when we went swimming as children.

I cried and cried and cried until no more tears would come. I had a migraine from crying so much. I had a tightness in my chest, and I felt like I was dying inside. My body felt numb. I went through the entire spectrum of emotions a 16-year-old can experience, from shock to disbelief, to anger, and sadness. In this frame of mind, you start questioning everything and blaming everyone.

I remember my boyfriend trying to take away the sadness in any way he possibly could. I was resting on his chest as he was caressing my long hair with his hand while the other hand was on my back. He was providing much-needed comfort. As I listened closely, I could hear his heartbeat. This triggered me. I remember thinking, how can it be fair that my brother's heart stopped beating? He was so young, and his life had barely started. I questioned my faith, God, the universe, and all the beliefs I had at the time. Why me? What did I ever do to deserve this pain? Teenage years can be challenging enough. I did not need an added challenge to overcome.

When I went back to school, it was highly recommended for my brother's close friends and family members to meet with the school therapist to discuss the grieving process and the five stages of grief. I remember the therapist talking to me, but all I could see were her lips moving. I was not tuning in to any of the words she was saying. I was tired of people acting differently around me. Tired of feeling like the world had stopped and I was stuck navigating through dark times for what seemed like an eternity, even though it had only been a couple of days. Tired of people who had not even experienced grief themselves telling me how to grieve—tired of complicated processes to suffer. My life did not pause because my brother passed away. I had school, friends, sports, activities, a job, homework, and wanted to obtain good grades to attend university. All I wanted to do was to find a solution to heal my profound sadness. As a teenager, the only thing I knew how to do was how to comfort my sorrow with music, go within, and find stillness in my heart. That is when I discovered that gratitude could assist in grieving the loss of a loved one.

After much reflection, I understood that gratitude was an option. Staying paralyzed in a storm of sadness was also a choice. I could decide to try some coping mechanisms that would help me navigate through the hard times or stay stuck in a whirlwind of emotions. Life provides endless options, and every day offers a conscious choice to cope differently. I knew in my heart that the things that try to knock me down, eventually, make me stronger. I rise from obstacles, and that is how I grow my resilience. To me, choosing the path of gratitude was a simple choice. There were no other alternatives. I wanted the path to acceptance and healing as quickly as possible. I wanted to go on with my life, but I knew it would be changed forever. There was no going back to the life I previously had, as it no longer existed. I had to let go of how others expected me to grieve and find a way to heal at my own pace.

In the next section, I am inviting you to look at the five coping tips I used in my healing journey: a positive mindset, a gratitude journal, affirmations, a gratitude jar, and a gratitude letter.

Positive Mindset

When you notice your mind shifting to a negative space, acknowledge it, release it, and move your awareness back to a positive mindset. When you ask yourself questions that are triggering emotions of anger, guilt, blame, or even sadness, change your questions from:

- Why him?

- Why couldn't anyone save him?

- Why is life so unfair?

- Why do I have to go through so much pain?

- What did I ever do to deserve this hardship?

To:

- What lesson can I learn from this experience?

- How can I grow?

- How can this difficult and challenging experience make me stronger and more resilient?

- What does this pain teach me?

- What can I do to bring some positivity to my day?

Gratitude Journal and Affirmations:

If you are new to writing in a journal, place your pen on a blank page and start writing positive statements like: "I am grateful for...," "I am...," "Today is ..." The more you practice the art of writing in a gratitude journal, the more words will flow effortlessly on the paper. Feel the emotion of gratitude flood your heart while you are writing. I recommend doing this first thing in the morning.

The goal is to write at least five things per day, then move up to ten items. It can even be one or two words, but the key is to write. For this method to be effective, you need to be consistent and try to write in it every day. If one day you lack inspiration, you can read the previous pages of your journal entries. It will create a momentum of positivity and empowering thoughts. It can then inspire you to write. The more you elaborate on your thoughts, the easier it will become to journal. Be as specific as you can. It may be challenging at first, but it will become more comfortable as you practice this every day. Write in the present tense, and make sure the statements are positive. Feel every emotion, and try to put them into words in your journal. Try to dig deep and let your heart guide your pen. If words don't come out, write anything you would like to become. For example, if you lack sleep, you can write: "I am well-rested. I have an abundance of energy today."

The main difference between a gratitude journal and affirmations is that a gratitude journal will explain something positive which happened during the day, while affirmations are empowering statements to start your day with a positive mindset.

Generally, a gratitude journal and daily affirmations should be done separately. Still, when you are grieving the loss of a loved one, sometimes it can be challenging to find something you are grateful for, especially if you are new at journaling. I find it easier to combine both items in the same journal. If you are a seasoned professional at keeping a daily routine of writing in a gratitude journal and affirmations, keep on doing them separately. There is no right or wrong way of journaling during a period of grief and sorrow. The goal is to write some positive words on paper, which will help you let go of your heart's sadness. When you are writing about the good things, the happy moments in your day, you are giving yourself permission to rewire your brain. Scientific research has proven that it is impossible to be grateful and sad at the same time.

Here are some examples of items you can write about in a gratitude journal:

- I am grateful to have a sister who understands my pain, feels my sadness, and grieves with me.

- I am not alone.

- I am grateful for the school principal understanding my grief and not requiring me to attend classes until I am ready to return to school.

- I am grateful for the beautiful memories I have of my loved ones.

- I am grateful for my health.

- I am grateful for the sun rising this morning.

- I am thankful to have so many friends who love me and offer their assistance.

- I am stronger than the person I was yesterday.

- I am resilient to obstacles and challenges.

- I am stronger than any storm.

- I am capable of anything.

- I do not let outside circumstances I cannot control disrupt my inner peace.

- I let go of things I cannot control.

- I enjoy every moment.

- I am no longer holding on to the pain of yesterday.

- I overcome all obstacles that stand in my way to achieving greatness.

- I permit myself to smile again.

- I give myself permission to laugh again.

- I create happy memories every day.

- I am loved.

- I choose how I feel.

- I choose to be happy.

- Today is a beautiful day.

- Today, I choose to heal at my own pace.

- I do my best every day.

- I am proud of myself.

- My story inspires others.

Gratitude Jar:

- Choose a clear glass jar, decorate it, and make it beautiful.

- Place it in a location in your home where you will see it every day.

- Take a small piece of paper, and write one thing that you are grateful for each day.

- Fold the paper in half and place it in the jar.

You will see the jar fill up quickly. Every time you walk past the gratitude jar, your heart will instantly open up, and you will feel a massive jolt of appreciation and gratitude. Never underestimate the healing ability the gratitude jar can provide. It will immediately initiate happy memories.

If you struggle with what to write on the paper, think about:

- What made you laugh or smile today?

- What or who inspired you today?

- What is something magical that happened today?

- What obstacle did you overcome today?

- What are you thankful for today?

- What makes you happy?

Gratitude Letter:

Write a gratitude letter to someone you love or appreciate by speaking with your heart. The gratitude letter can even be addressed to the person who passed away if you feel this would heal you. Don't question what you are writing. Just go within, and write everything that comes to your mind. Don't let your mind filter your thoughts; rather, try to feel every word and every emotion with your open heart.

This is an example of a gratitude letter I wrote to my twin sister after the passing of my brother:

Hi Melanie,

You are my womb mate, my twin sister, and my best friend. When I look at you, it feels like I am looking in the mirror because you are my exact reflection. Your inner beauty radiates outwards. You understand me without the need to speak. You have a sense of just knowing. You never judge me, and you hold a safe space for me filled with unconditional love. We have a special bond that is rarely shared with anyone else. I am grateful to navigate this journey called life with you.

We have lived through the ups and downs of life together. Your smile is contagious. and it can light up a room. At the moment, your smile is gone. I see your shock and sadness. Your eyes are so piercing blue with so much light in them that they can see right to my soul, but at the moment, they are red from excessive crying. The light in your eyes is gone. I feel your profound sadness, your numbness, and your emptiness. Coping with our brother's sudden loss is the most challenging situation we have had to face so far in life. I understand the unfairness of all of this, as he had so many unaccomplished dreams.

We are strong and resilient, and this is our time to become even stronger than ever before. Strength comes from adversity. We have known this our whole lives. Together, we can get through everything. We always have. We can get through this... one day at a time.

Thank you for being in my life. I appreciate every moment with you. If I didn't have you as my twin sister, I would choose you as my best friend. Thank you.

Love always,

Julie

Letter Writing tips:

- It can be any length, but it needs to be authentic, sincere, and come from the heart.

- Explain why you are thankful and appreciate this person in your life.

- End the letter with a closing statement, and sign the letter.

The more you practice these five coping tips: a positive mindset, a gratitude journal, affirmations, a gratitude jar and a gratitude letter, the easier it will become to shift your emotions from sadness to happiness.

Life is so short and precious. Make every single day count. Enjoy every moment of love, joy, and happiness. Make gratitude become part of your everyday life. As Robert A. Emmons points out: "Opening ourselves to the majestic moments in our lives naturally redirects our attention to the gifts that surround us" (P. 4).

Christina Rasmussen, a crisis-intervention specialist, coach, and speaker, states in her book, Second Firsts: "Grief opens your heart so you can undergo transformation. But it is up to you to take this expansion and spread it everywhere in your life (P. 37) [...] Your grief is not here to end your life and destroy your soul, but to bring you back to life. Your grief is not here to punish you, but to teach you how to live. It's here to set you free"(P. 58).

When you start viewing life through the lens of gratitude, your mindset shifts immediately to appreciate the beauty this world offers. Gratitude can redirect your focal point to a positive mindset. You acknowledge your strength, develop your resilience through adversity, and you have an increased dose of courage to keep moving forward in life despite the hard times. Gratitude changes your perception, and it forces you to look within your heart where you can find a deeper meaning of life.

We often avoid discussing coping mechanisms for grieving the loss of a loved one because it is a difficult topic to address. Some people fear death—they are afraid to cry or to show weakness. Unfortunately, death is inevitable. Give yourself the time and the permission to grieve. Share your knowledge by offering coping tips to others.

If you know someone going through the painful loss of a loved one, and if you want to help them by giving them tools to navigate this challenging time, provide them with this book. It is not always easy to find the words to say to a loved one going through the grieving process, but it is essential to reach out to them and show them that you care and can provide support.

From my personal experience, the most effective way to grieve the loss of a loved one is by keeping it simple and practicing the art of gratitude consistently every single day. The emptiness you feel inside will eventually subside and be replaced by love, joy, happiness, and appreciation. Grieving is a personal journey and gratitude has helped me immensely. It is powerful beyond measure. The invisible healing benefit of appreciation has the ability to bring comfort in the wave of sadness and hope in a time of despair.

Permit yourself to grieve. Take the time to heal your mind, body, and soul. Start living, laughing, and smiling again. I know that my mother and brother would want me to celebrate their lives and focus on the happy times, not dwell on the pain of their passing. Love is infinite and eternal and if we simply recall and cherish our happy memories together, we can connect with them again. When you bring your awareness back to the present moment and use the coping tips discussed in this chapter, you are giving yourself permission to move forward from grief and start the healing process.

I hope that sharing my journey of losing both my brother and my mother at such a young age has inspired you to try the coping mechanisms described in this chapter. Include gratitude in your everyday life, and become the best version of yourself. There's no reason to wait until you're grieving to start being grateful. When you open your heart every morning and genuinely appreciate all the beauty in your life, your mind will start focusing only on the positive things in life.

When mourning the loss of a loved one, please remember:

Grief can paralyze you and keep you stuck in the corridor of loss, but gratitude is the key to releasing the tidal wave of sadness and replacing it with healing and acceptance. Gratitude will enable you to rise above the darkness and bloom like a lotus flower. The path of gratitude is the solution to finding the light in a time of profound darkness.

"Let us be grateful to the people who make us happy. They are the charming gardeners who make our souls blossom."

~ Marcel Proust

CHAPTER THREE

Moments of Reflection in Gratitude

By Kylie de Mole

"I choose to live with gratitude for the love that fills my heart, the peace that rests within my spirit, and the voice of hope that says all things are possible."

~ Anonymous

A ll I ever did was work and exercise. There was no real meaning to my life other than work, some more work, two beautiful kitties, and my new hubby. But all I ever knew was work of some form. Recently a friend and I had done some goddess workaround reconnecting with my neglected inner child. From doing so, I had the grand idea that we should go for a trail ride when in Port Douglas on our upcoming family holiday. Growing up in the country, I'd had horses, Dusty and Fleur, and I still hold dear memories of them seeing me through the tough times of being a teenager.

Shane, my husband, organized the most beautiful trail ride through the Daintree and along Cape Tribulation. I made a joke to the person running the trail ride: "You watch. I will go home and call you to buy this horse and bring her home to Melbourne." Funnily enough, he declined my offer.

We came home, and I started looking at horses for sale. I had in mind that I would buy a well-educated safe horse that I could just trail ride with, although in my heart I had the idea I wanted to get a horse that I could grow with—quite a silly idea considering that, apart from the recent trail ride, I had not been on a horse for about 25 years.

I found my fairy tale dream horse. He was black and magnificent—my Black Beauty, just what I had always dreamed of riding. We were due to see him and hopefully organize to bring him home, although the owner kept putting us off again and again, saying he needed another week with the trainer. The night before the day we were meant to pick up Koda, we received another message: He is not ready yet. My heart sunk. Patience, at this point, had never really been my greatest strength.

I got back onto Facebook Marketplace just to have another look at what was about. "Just looking," I explained to hubby. I saw pictures of a horse that looked withdrawn and sad, and his name was Rusty. My favorite horse ever had been Dusty. It was just too close in the name for me to ignore. I sent a message and asked if I could come to visit the next afternoon. I thought to myself, *if it's meant to be, it will be. If she said yes, we would go cheer him up and take some apples. If no, well, that's what it is.* Shane was quick to point out that it's a long way to cheer up a horse, so I quickly turned it around and said, "Let's just go for a drive. You love driving!"

We drove four hours, and as we pulled up, I had a feeling that I'd never felt before rush through my whole body. I could see this chestnut horse in the distance. I said to Shane, "It's him!" He looked at me and said, "Hun, we are only here to visit." I said again, swallowing back the tears, "It's him."

We spent time meeting Rusty. He was shy. He felt quite reserved, shut down even, but his eyes felt familiar. I had a sense that we were reuniting, as crazy as that sounds.

I told the guy I would take him, and, on the spot, I transferred the $300, plus $200 for transporting him to Melbourne, with instructions to get him down to me the following Saturday. I just went with it, having no idea what was next.

Rusty arrived in Melbourne on the 26th of November 2016. All I had was a paddock at an agistment close to home, some chaff, and a heart ready to love him. My parents came to meet him that afternoon, and I couldn't even catch him once he was in his paddock. After about an hour, I walked him down to meet my mum and dad. My dad, an animal lover who had grown up with horses and had helped me in my younger years, took one look and said to me, "Kylie, he needs a good drench and a lot of tender, loving care."

My mum, being the faithful soul she is, said, "Don't worry, Michael. She will sort him out."

I spent the next few weeks feeding him up and relearning everything. The agistment was a riding school, so there were plenty of people around with knowledge and a willingness to offer help. Some advice was welcomed, and some was unwelcomed. It got incredibly hard for us there. I realized there were much bigger issues at play with Rusty than what I could pinpoint. Even though there were some beautiful people at the riding school, the environment we were in felt harsh and carried the wrong energy.

I ended up stumbling across a new agistment for us on my work travels. I went through the large black gates at the front, which were a little intimidating at first. It looked pretty fancy, but I went in anyway. The owner was not available, so I left my details, got her mobile number, and later called and asked about availability.

Shane and I went and met with the owner that weekend. Driving around the property, Shane and I both felt quite safe with her and decided to move Rusty there. After we explained our situation and lack of knowledge, Jill was incredibly kind and offered to come and pick us up to move Rusty in within the month.

That month, waiting to move was a real struggle. Rusty was slowly getting stronger and fatter with a better diet, loads of loving, and consistent food. I couldn't really ride, because I didn't know how to other than galloping along the beach as I had done 25 years ago or walk. I knew the basics but kept things simple. We would just walk about bareback (in hindsight, completely insane of me) and, at times, in our brand-new saddle, which was uncomfortable for the both of us. Rusty's personality and cheekiness were really starting to come out, which was heart-warming. With my lack of horse knowledge, I was beginning to feel like I was drowning, although I somehow continued to have a complete sense of gratitude that we had come together. I would often sit and watch him eat his dinner while promising him I would give this my all and do what I could to heal his past. I was determined to stay positive and do what I could, even knowing I was way out of my depth.

We moved into the new agistment around a month later. When Jill picked us up, she took one look at him and realized Rusty wasn't in the best condition and that we all needed some expert support. After we arrived at our new home, we unloaded what seemed like a fire-breathing red dragon, and I walked him around the property and down to his new paddock. The best way to describe what I was walking is a highflying kite in the form of a farting and snorting dragon weighing over 400 kilos. My heart was beating a million miles a minute, but inside I was falling apart. I loved him so much, but all I knew was that I just needed to keep breathing, keep calm, and keep my naturally positive disposition.

On unpacking the car and Rusty's gear, one of the girls at the agistment came up to me and abruptly shouted, "I just thought I'd let you know, green on green equals black. You don't have a clue."

I was dumbfounded and just smiled at her and walked off. I walked back down to our new paddock and hid in Rusty's shelter and just cried, curled up in a ball. I knew what she was referring to. A green (new) horse with a green (new) rider was a tragedy waiting to happen, a complete disaster ending with one of us dead, broken, or black and bruised. It was hard at a soul level. I felt sick with fear and just so incredibly alone and frightened. It was terrifying. Here was this most magnificent creature, a powerhouse that had already had a hard start to life, who was frightened of everything bar Shane and me. He was getting fitter and stronger physically. He would need to work, and it would have to be the correct work, too;

otherwise he would be a danger not only to himself but also to others and us.

This was the moment that I realized what I had done was completely ridiculous. Buying a horse—a green horse—at my age with no experience. It all hit me hard with the realization of the complete stupidity of my crazy idea, but what was I going to do? Was I way too invested at this point?

Rusty obviously felt something was wrong and came up, gently nuzzling me. I apologized to him for not knowing more and for getting us both into this mess. He just stood there staring at me, as if he were staring straight through me, and stood there with his massive big eyes as if to tell me it was going to be okay, that he trusted me.

As they say, you need to have a break down to have a breakthrough. This was mine. I thought I'd had my share of them in my life, but this one tried hard to break me and my heart.

I'm not a quitter, never have been, but I was so far out of my depth. This would have to have been the craziest thing I had ever done in my 41 cycles around the sun, and at this stage, we were only three months into our journey.

In the following weeks, when I was in tie-ups with Rusty, Jill, who had been like a fairy godmother to us so far, came up to me and mentioned Belle, her riding coach. She had noticed we had tried a couple of other coaches and had no luck with them. Jill said Belle was quite busy and not taking on new clients, but she may be worth talking to as she has many years of experience in both her personal and professional career and would probably like to help me.

I had seen this lady about teaching others, and with her new little puppy there was something that drew me to her, but we'd never had the chance to talk. I had this internal fear that she would tell me green on green equals black and confirm how stupid I had been. I needed to block out all the judgments others were passing at us and stay positive and internally focused.

I ran into Belle. Her little puppy, Axle, had run up to say hi, so I was having a little chat and cuddle with him as she approached. We had a brief interaction about him and his boldness. I tried to get the courage to ask her for help, but for some reason, fear ate my words. I knew I was better than this and needed to get over myself and do what I had promised Rusty I would do.

A few days later, I saw Belle and little Axle and went up to her to say hi. Instead, I blurted out like a child, "I need help. Please help us. I can't keep kidding myself." At this stage, I was desperate. That week Rusty had taken off while I was putting on his rug, almost running through the fence. The rug had gone flying, frightening him even more, and then it had covered his face, flapping in the wind while he bolted around his paddock. Finally, he let me near him to take what was left of the rug off him. It seemed like hours. I'm not sure it could have gotten any worse at this point. I had spent the night in his shelter, as he was completely trembling in fear from his rug incident, and his nose was bleeding everywhere. The vet told me not to worry, but I found it impossible not to. It had been a couple of weeks from hell. I was desperate.

Belle could see and feel it and just looked at me and said, "Sure, when are you free? Does Saturday suit?" We pretty much booked a lesson then and there for the next day. She had seen and felt our struggle.

I don't have the words to express the gratitude I have for this woman. There aren't words to describe what she means to Shane, Rusty, and me. Belle has been by our side ever since, and still is to this day. It certainly hasn't been without a struggle, and for a while there, it seemed to worsen, but we were no longer alone on the journey. We had found our person and, at that point, our home.

From the first lesson, Belle taught us groundwork and taught me about Rusty's background as a Standardbred horse, about harness racing, and about his fears. She helped me train him to be confident and brave. This was our biggest focus.

Our first few lessons seemed to go on for hours. Belle was committed and passionate about helping us. She could sense we both had the heart to make this work and did everything she could to support us.

A few weeks into our time together, she was honest with me and said, "Kylie, I need to tell you, Rusty isn't actually broken to saddle." To which I replied, "So, green on green does equal black."

I will never forget her response.

"Definitely not in this case. You two have a bond that's rare. You are meant to be together."

I burst into tears. It was as if she literally removed the burden sitting in the pit of my heart. And I finally knew that we were going to be okay under her guidance.

We went on to discuss our options to send him off and have him broken in properly. Belle sternly replied to me, "NO, no, you can do it; he will never forgive you if you send him off now. You're the only one he trusts."

"WHAT! I can't do it. I have no idea what the hell I'm doing."

She said bluntly, "You'll be fine. You can do it."

I wasn't sure what planet she was from, but she was one of the only people I trusted at this point, and I knew I had to listen and follow her guidance, as it was the support that I had begged for so many times over.

Belle certainly had her work cut out. We were both blank slates and new to it all. I had an unrelenting determination to learn, grow, and be the best human I could be for Rusty, so we all worked hard to get us where we needed to be to build strong foundations. We started with the basics and just kept going. The bond between us kept growing, and the trust between us was becoming an unspoken inner knowing. Belle had me working hard to teach Rusty to be brave and to make it safe for him to be confident, to believe in himself, all while teaching me to have confidence in myself.

No matter how naughty Rusty became in his newfound body of strength and power, I still felt safe. We made tremendous progress. Although there were days that felt like we would take ten steps forward and thirteen steps back, we kept going and pushing through. Rusty's newfound strength and self-confidence caused him to move at times between a bouncing horse inspired by Pepe Le Pew and a horse auditioning for the local rodeo with me as the rodeo clown sitting on top. For whatever crazy reason within me, I never felt the fear that he was trying to hurt me or get me off, but rather, that he was excitable, testing his newly found muscles and agility. Belle coached me through his naughtiness, teaching me to sit and ride it out. I often heard the words "Think of your bum as a sack of potatoes" or her telling me to sit there like I'm a Buddha. Belle often said things like, "Legs on!" and "You've got this. YOU can do this." She never gave up on the duo that is Rusty and Kylie.

I cannot say this was always the way. There was an incident where things went really wrong. One night when Rusty took off like a rocket ship, launching a million miles into space, I went flying, still holding on to the reins and bringing him down on top of me. At this stage, his 500 kilos falling on top of my relatively smallish frame certainly hurt, to say the least, smacking me hard into the ground. Thankfully, we were on the sand and there were no major injuries to either of us: luckily enough, only a mild concussion and vertigo for me. After a thorough check-over, we found that Rusty was completely fine. We were both just shaken up, but this was a massive lesson for us both and again deepened that unspoken bond that we had developed. Now, if I almost fall off due to some of his, let us say, fresh, excitable behavior, he catches my fall. I don't understand how, but every time he manages to save me from my fall. In addition, it is now my job to ensure I do what I can not to fall. It was another of what they call a defining moment in our relationship—taking it to another level, as lessons tend to do.

I have certainly made plenty of mistakes along the way, for sure. Going to a dressage competition early on in the piece—now that was incredibly humbling and incredibly humiliating. The judge even said to us at the end of the test, "Are you sure you are in the right place? This is not a rodeo." It did not help that we got a standing ovation for me merely staying on and that someone yelled out to me, "Go get 'em, cowgirl!" Did I mention that this was a dressage competition, not a rodeo? The whole time we were there, Rusty either looked like aliens were trying to beam him up by his head or he was bucking up and down on the spot. This was one of our worst days. We had a long way to go before we were to venture out again.

Back home, we began to rework and work hard at sorting ourselves out. We learned a hard lesson that day, which was to not get ahead of ourselves and to not let our egos cause us to let others influence us too much. We learned to actually step back and to ensure we were always in gratitude and to remember why we started on our journey together. It is a day I often reflect on, even now, to make sure I am not getting ahead of myself and letting my ego overtake where we are. I need to remember humility in our work, to help Rusty stay brave and keep the two of us in gratitude at all times as a team.

We continue to work hard with Belle every weekend without fail. We have a riding lesson, and sometimes two, as we stay true to the promise I made to Rusty. Belle works with us tirelessly, teaching me how to become a dressage rider, all the while teaching Rusty how to use his body correctly to ensure he is strong and looked after in the best possible way.

We take time of rest, giving us both a break from the steep learning curve we're on. Through those rest times we go for walks as I let Rusty pick at the fresh grass for hours while I sit there watching him. Rusty and I stay consistent in our learnings and work hard every day to ensure we are both safe.

As time progressed, I started revisiting our bareback riding. There was an inner sense for us to go back to that. It felt safe to enter this space. It no longer felt like the insane idea it was in the beginning. Without the realization of doing so, I was creating a safe space for us when bareback riding, a time for us both to be still. It was like a restorative yoga meditation class but bareback, just Rusty and me. For a time, this was an imperative part of our weekly training and a great chance to reflect and listen to wholesome music.

Unfortunately, this was changed when we had an accident around 18 months before writing this piece. Rusty fell over while scrambling and losing his legs in the horse float several times, slicing his back with three long lashes across it. The center divider came out and was stuck across his back. As he got up, it sliced across once again and then was stuck on his back for the third time.

I thought I had faced the hardest of challenges to date in our journey, but I was so wrong. Getting Rusty up and out of the float that was now stuck and bent inward and then walking him up a main road to get him home was undoubtedly the hardest challenge yet, and certainly the most heart-wrenching. As any horse owner, including me, will tell you, this is what nightmares are made of. My heart still trembles when I think back to that day.

The back of the horse float had bent inward. Despite everything Shane and I did, we could not get it to budge. Once we got Rusty safely up and standing, I stood calming him, while Shane worked at somehow trying to get us out. It was hot and getting stuffy inside. Rusty wouldn't let me move without ensuring his body was touching mine somehow, staying really close, making it harder for me to assist Shane to move the twisted latch. I got Shane to call someone to come and help us out. Then I had to stand with Rusty while I checked over his back to see if I could help his wounds. Standing behind Rusty, I was desperately trying to wriggle the latch out, and, at the same time, Rusty pushed his back end into me and with his body weight pushed me into the bent latch. Somehow I was able to pull it out and the back breaching doors flew open. I still claim to this day that it was some form of miracle, and divine guidance was by our side.

I'll never forget the sense of relief rushing through me. We got Rusty off the float, but as he got out—if things were not bad enough—we had unknowingly parked next to a paddock full of llamas. Horses hate llamas. But he had to just deal with it and suck it up. He started snorting and, once again, I was desperately trying to calm my anxiety-driven, panicked, injured, fire-breathing red dragon. I had to walk him up a busy main road with trucks and cars coming at us to get him home so the vet could go to work on him straight away. He was walking without any lameness, so we felt it safer to get him home and off the main road, rather than stay where we were, which was far too dangerous.

I don't remember a lot from that day. It's all a bit of a blur. When I think back, tears of relief and gratefulness still come over me. I remember clearly bowing my head into Rusty, trembling on the float and saying aloud, "Please, God, help us. We need you. Please help us get back home safely."

Absolutely everything I had learned in life and on the ground with Belle was in play now. This was real and, in hindsight, I realize that these are the days you do the work for. I only had one chance to get him home safely. This was the most dangerous situation I'd ever found myself in. He was my responsibility and trusted me. It was time to finally prove to myself that I had this, that I was worthy of his trust and that I could keep him safe. I felt unstoppable. An unwavering amount of strength came surging through me. Cars were coming at us, and I had to yell at them to get out of our way. I was fraught with fear, but something clicked within me, and to this day I don't really know how I got him home as safely as I did. I felt a massive sense of relief as I walked him through the gates, and the vet was there within minutes.

The vet was quick to remind us how lucky we were, as generally with float accidents like ours, he would have been there to put the horse down. However, the cooling rug I had put on Rusty had saved him because it was slippery material. To be honest, there was a lot of divine guidance with us that day. It is hard to deny. Rusty would be okay and just needed time off to heal his back wounds. Knowing he was okay gave me a huge sense of relief.

Then the hard news came: He might not be ridable again, and, even if he would be rideable, it was doubtful I would ever be able to ride him bareback again.

Never underestimate the power of love and determination. Rusty recovered incredibly well with loads of TLC, bodywork, and strengthening work. Recently we have been gifted with the ability to ride bareback again.

It has certainly been a journey and one that keeps on keeping on.

We have had loads of obstacles and even more triumphs. We are finally building back up the courage to go out and compete. Surprisingly, we have won two big dressage jackpots. Who would have ever thought! We have come that far in the three and a half years we have been together.

Rusty, on both occasions, was a bigger champion than words could even describe. On one occasion, there was complete carnage. The winds were something movies are made of. When we were riding our tests, it felt as if we were Dorothy inside the tornado in *The Wizard of Oz*. With pieces of dressage arenas, bags, and anything else that had been lying about flying around us, these felt like 50k winds. It was insane. Belle said to me, "This is nothing but a test in trust. Forget everything other than your bond and keep him with you. Let him trust you to keep him safe." I did that. He stayed with me the whole time; he was calm and nothing less than brilliant, and he deserved the win and the champion status that day. WE DID IT. We had come full circle.

The challenges we have faced have been raw and personally confronting. The ability to stay positive and in gratitude has certainly helped ease the process. However, having the most amazing support team in Shane and Belle and some other fantastic women we've met along the way has been priceless.

There is an unspoken bond of love and gratitude between all of us: Shane, Belle, Rusty, and me. Belle is my confidant and very dear friend. "The best kind of people are the ones that come into your life and make you see the sun where you once saw clouds. The people that believe in you so much, you start to believe in you too. The people that love you simply for being you. The once in a lifetime kind of people." (Kate Lattey, Against the Clock: Clearwater Bay #2) This describes our super coach Belle undoubtedly, with the sun she brought into our lives the day she said yes to helping us. I am forever in gratitude to her.

Shane and Rusty have become the best of buddies and behave in the same way as two little 13-year-olds. The two of them have unshakable respect and love for each other. Rusty is often resting his head on Shane's shoulder and nuzzling into him as if he were a small puppy, not the 500-kilo powerhouse he has become.

As for Rusty and me, we have come so incredibly far in many ways. We still use our bareback rides to meditate and connect. We hang together, breathing in stillness, gentleness, and grace, words which describe my dear horse and best friend, Rusty. We trust in one another genuinely and have proven it repeatedly over again. We are a team working to be one. I am honored and proud he found me and believed in me to do right by him. He is my wings. He is my spirit, and I am his human. Together will continue to persevere in strengthening everything we have worked so hard for. Rusty is my greatest teacher—my teacher in patience, determination, unconditional love and gratitude.

> **"In the steady gaze of the horse shines a silent eloquence that speaks of love and loyalty, strength and courage. It is the window that reveals to us how willing is his spirit, how generous his heart."**
>
> ~Unknown

43

"Learn to be thankful for what you already have while you pursue all that you want."

~ Jim Rohn

CHAPTER FOUR

How Can Music Be Our Lifeline

By Simone Waddell

I am so grateful for MUSIC!

Music has been a thread that has woven through every stage of my life a gift from heaven that has inspired joy and happiness, regardless of circumstances.

Singing and songwriting have brought me countless wonderful opportunities; I have been blessed to travel the world performing with world class musicians in magnificent theatres and venues in China, Japan, the USA, Norway, and Australia, my homeland.

For a month in January 2018, I coached phenomenal African singers in Uganda, including the Watoto Children's Choir. In Africa, I was surrounded by people who were astonishingly generous but had very little material wealth. I witnessed their gratitude for life, and it had a profound impact on me.

> **"It is not joy that makes us grateful, it is gratitude that makes us joyful."**
>
> ~ David Steindl-Rast

Gratitude is a state of being, and the more I practice it, the better everything becomes.

I am honored to work with creative people every day, helping them truly find their amazing individual voice. For almost thirty years I have coached thousands of private voice and singing lessons and facilitated *YOU HAVE A VOICE* workshops. I have hosted retreats in stunning natural environments, with clear swimming pools, surrounded by rainforests, and with an abundance of healthy food, fresh air, and sunshine.

I teach that when you live the "Song of Your Life" and consciously align your highest beliefs, thoughts, words, and actions, you will soon discover that you are the greatest project you will ever work on. You owe it to yourself. Everyone around you will benefit when you become the person you have dreamed of being.

My life today is completely different from how it used to be, and for that, I am profoundly grateful.

For years, I was walking through a terrible, dark place, and my soul, spirit, and body were suffering from perpetual crisis and trauma. Through the power of gratitude, I was able to rise out of that dark place and be free, full of hope for the future.

Adversity offers many gifts, and a heart of gratefulness can be forged in the flames of anguish and suffering.

Here is some of my former reality—the dark times…

The year is 2003. It is a gorgeous, clear blue, Californian-December sky in the early afternoon. I can't remember the last time I ate or slept, can't bring myself to either.

There is a traumatized state, and then there is another deeper realm beyond that, where I am right now.

His red car drives down the street. I watch from the window.

He is gone. Hurry. Go. Move. Grab whatever you can and LEAVE.

Driving with his sister and grandmother to Los Angeles International Airport, I have an intense combination of terror and liberation.

I feel in my spirit that this day marks the road to my freedom. *What if he finds out and punishes me again before I arrive? What if he chases us? What if the flight is delayed?*

I was going to tell him the night before. I have no poker face. I am honest. Submissive. Obedient. I am a good Christian wife. So, I'll tell him I'm leaving. I'll tell him.

The abuse is too much. I need to go, and I will keep praying that he will stop the abuse.

The main elements in an abused Christian wife's tool kit are fasting and praying.

Pray harder. Obey. Be quiet.

If people knew that the only option that works when dealing with a hardened abuser with no conscience is a process called:

"Run for the hills and never look back, in Jesus name. Amen."

"And how do you think that night will pan out once you tell him?" asks his Mother, who is also no stranger to violent men, and had to admit her own son was one. She is right. I cannot tell him.

I leave so much behind. A baby and a suitcase are all I can take.

At the airport, one hour away, my case is overweight, and I am asked to pay for excess baggage.

I begin the undignified scramble to open the case on the ground. I'm barely holding on by a thread, and now I am somehow juggling the contents between my carry-on and my suitcase adhering to the rules and not pay for the excess.

It is nearly midnight, way past Caleb's* bedtime. My baby. He is 18 months old. Pure, precious joy.

Then, I hear the announcement. That which I feared has come upon me. The flight is delayed by one hour. He can get here within that time. This is terror...

Finally, the hour passes in a blur. We get on the plane. *Another* delay is announced. An elderly man assigned to sit next to us is furious, furious to be next to a baby. He says the word *baby* like it is poison. He is loudly demanding to be moved elsewhere and is barking sarcastic and rude taunts at me and my child. The staff accommodate his wishes. Surrounding passengers chastise him for his unprovoked cruelty. What more? God. What more?

Another elderly man is moved next to us. He adores Caleb immediately. He is like a long-lost Grandpa, kind and compassionate.

I feel relieved and grateful in my sheer exhaustion.

Travelling alone on an interstate flight with a toddler is often quite demanding; travelling like this to escape years of domestic violence is a whole new level of challenge.

The phone call to my Mom was brief. I am in the USA, in California. My parents are in Sydney, Australia.

"Do you remember the time I told you I was being abused early in the marriage? It never stopped. I have been abused the whole time... We have to escape; we cannot stay. Caleb and I will be at the airport in Sydney at 6:30am on December 4th. Please be there. I have to go now. I cannot stay on the phone."

Surely that is a phone call no mother or grandmother ever wants to receive.

I had always done well in school. I won a scholarship to attend an incredible music college in America. I have loving, supportive parents and friends. I had a promising music career ahead of me. How did I end up here?

Why am I in *this?* I am being abused. This is abuse.

I am brainwashed.

How fortunate that I am married to a Christian man, I try to convince myself, again.

How is it possible? A missionary? A *"Man of God?"*

We were in Japan to serve the church. Enrique* prepared sermons and preached every Sunday. He knew the Bible. However, as William Shakespeare rightly said, *"The Devil can cite scripture for his purpose."*

And "devil" is not too strong a word.

A split personality who played the role of my own personal terrorist—ruling and controlling all aspects of my existence. He caused more harm than any narrative could express. His sense of entitlement as my lord and master was staggering. On one occasion, I was punished mercilessly because I wore an outfit, and he screamed, "I can see your arms!"

Deprivation of sleep and food exacerbated a 'walking on eggshells' existence. Enrique vacillated between stonewalling silent treatment and aggressive, drawn out rages.

To the outside world, he was almost an angel. Behind closed doors, his opposite persona practiced an ongoing repertoire of verbal, psychological, sexual, physical, emotional, and financial abuse, all held solidly in place by enormous spiritual abuse.

His litany was often repeated:

"I hate you. I would rather be dead than be married to you. I have to punish you. No one would ever want you. Anyone would be better than you. I hate you more than anyone I have ever met. You need to tell people you will never work again and never sing again."

I was called a dog, a mutt, fat, ugly, and hundreds of other insults, accompanied by swearing and profanity. The sexual abuse was overt, like the rest of his cruel and tormenting ways. The tirades and abusive episodes often lasted all night.

The nearby Buddhist temple would ring their bell at sunrise. I could not count the amount of times I was abused all night and he was still raging and tormenting me when the temple bell rang the next morning.

I had been yelled at, sworn at, shoved, pushed, thrown against a set of wooden stairs, threatened, and deprived of opinions, choices, a driver's license, money, and clothes. My belongings were thrown and given away without my consent, repeatedly. I was humiliated, mocked, degraded, raped, and violated. I was falsely accused of perpetual affairs, forbidden from having contact with family and friends, and kept awake to endure all night tirades countless times. I was blamed continually.

I was lied to more times than I could say. Smear campaigns so horrendous I had no method of even processing the levels of cruelty.

The hypocrisy of this 'sober' missionary was incredible. I frequently found empty cans and bottles of alcohol hidden in cupboards, under the bed, or in the trunk of the car. And on Sundays, he preached in church that drinking was evil. A monstrous dichotomy.

Before my marriage, I ran ten kilometers a day. Once married and for a long while, I was forbidden to exercise. The first time I dressed to go for a run in Japan, I was threatened, sworn at, and blocked from leaving. We had been married only a few weeks.

I was isolated, alone, and living with someone who behaved in chronically wicked ways. I had never encountered such venom.

"Love does not claim possession but gives freedom."

~ Rabindranath Tagore

My own father is a gentleman and a gentle man. He is very kind and does not yell, swear, or raise his voice at anyone, so Enrique's behavior was foreign to me, yet I stayed. That's what good Christian wives do… right?

In 2001, while still living with Enrique in Japan, I became pregnant. I fell to my knees and prayed from my heart that I would be the mother this baby required, and that I would raise him with everything I had.

When the morning sickness began, it was unrelenting, and in the sixth week of pregnancy, I awoke with excruciating pain in my left leg. I immediately knew it was a deep vein thrombosis (DVT) because I had experienced this exact pain before at age eighteen and was hospitalized at the time. I went straight to the Red Cross Hospital in Nagano, Japan.

After a long series of events including ambulances, six painful weeks in ICU, intravenous drips, ultrasounds, my organs shutting down, constant requests from the Japanese doctors and surgeons for me to have an abortion, and an emergency trip to Tokyo on the Shinkansen (bullet train), I made it clear all round that I was going to proceed with the pregnancy, and if I die, I die.

"You are committing suicide if you have this baby" was the phrase often used by the doctors, who were truly doing their best to save my life. During this time in ICU, my husband was accusing me of faking the entire illness and "only doing all this for attention." He continued to torment me even whilst in the hospital.

I simply had faith that God would have his way. I related so much to this idea:

"To me, finding my faith, right now where I'm at, is putting all of my trust in something bigger than myself, and living for something bigger than myself and trying to do that through service."

~ Noor Tagouri

My mum and best friend, Rachelle, flew to Japan on a last-minute flight when I was in intensive care. I was so grateful to see them walk into my hospital room. Their kindness and love were palpable. They both saw what was happening. Rachelle noted this:

"That trip... I thought I was saying goodbye. When I arrived to you in the hospital you looked like an end of life patient. Your spirit was strong, but your body was failing. So many drugs being surged through your systems too. It was the most worrying time of my life, I'd say. It was surreal joking and laughing with you, knowing how sick you were. Your humor withstanding all. And, it was the first time I became aware that your then husband was extremely unusual—the state of your house after you had been in hospital for weeks was a shock—cans of beer littered all over your house at home but the hour-long manic religious rants at random. His abuse of your beautiful mum. We were reeling at home and freaking out in the hospital. I became very concerned that nothing was as it seemed. He was certainly not the man we had met in Australia. The worry caused knots of anxiety in my stomach and I dropped five kilos in a week. At the airport, I burst into tears, and the airline staff were so kind that they blocked out a row of seats for me to travel uninterrupted. The world had just cracked. I

52

*bawled most of the way home, and we were all
worried sick for months."*

It was a conscious step of faith to reject the advice of the doctors
and go ahead with the pregnancy, knowing it could be a fatal
decision. Amazingly, every ultrasound in the Japanese hospitals to
check the baby's heartbeat showed a stronger than average
response. A loud, pumping, undeniable heartbeat. I had resigned
myself to the fact that I may die, the baby may die, or the baby
may have multiple ongoing issues at best.

The doctors would comment on how unexpected it was for a baby
to have such a powerful heartbeat. This is a little warrior in my
tummy, no doubt in my mind.

**"It is the most powerful creation to have life
growing inside you.
There is no bigger gift."**

~ Beyonce

After much difficulty, I was allowed on a flight back to Australia,
and after some time in a hospital in Sydney, I was released and
began self-injecting twice a day with high doses of blood thinning
medication. The injections caused painful bruises.

I ended up in a wheelchair for a while.

The abuse continued.

It is hard to fathom how ANYONE can abuse a person who is on
the verge of dying. A person they married and vowed to love, who
is also carrying their unborn child.

Who is capable of such horror?

It seemed there was no line he would not cross.

I felt a churning, anxious feeling when I first met Enrique. I was on contract as a professional singer and pianist in a beautiful five-star hotel in Nagano, Japan. The contract was an absolute dream come true.

I was twenty-two, and I had no emotional resources to deal with manipulation at the level Enrique used, so I was easy prey. Plus, he kept claiming his faith in God, and that was an important value for me. His actions did not match his words by any stretch; however, I was rendered voiceless very quickly and was soon unable to even make a decision on my own.

If God told you to marry me and that I am the ONE, who am I to argue that? I do wonder, just quietly, why didn't God tell ME that? I thought to myself.

I was full of dread the night before the wedding. I walked down the aisle in front of my beloved family and friends in a beautiful wedding gown. Glorious flowers were on display throughout the church and wonderful music played, yet I saw disdain and contempt on the face of my groom.

Due to abuse I experienced in childhood from my extended family, I already had a belief that I had to always agree to keep the peace. Boundaries are a foreign concept to people who have been abused, and it takes diligent effort and an awakening to learn what they are and how to implement them.

I knew my marriage was unsafe, yet I truly *believed* I had to stay and keep trying and praying… while my soul eroded more and more every day. I also felt terrible shame that I had made such a shocking decision, that I had ignored my own intuition, that I had ended up in such a horror story. I felt a constant unrest in my soul and spirit while my husband was loose and irresponsible with money, time, his word, and the truth.

Caleb was born in Sydney in May 2002, alive, well, and strong. The Japanese doctors, when they learned of the successful birth, called him "Miracle Caleb!" It was a long road working with the

RAP Team—Risk Associated Pregnancy. The pregnancy, labor, and the years beyond were not without complications, but we made it! Caleb's safe arrival is one of the most treasured moments of immense gratitude that I have ever known. This beautiful boy, this gift from heaven.

"So, there's this boy. He kind of stole my heart. He calls me "Mom.""

~ Unknown

When Caleb was eight months old, I succumbed to pressure from Enrique to travel to the USA where his family lived. Doctors in Sydney strongly advised against the trip as I had not recovered. I felt I had no option in the matter, and the punishments I would inevitably receive to decline the trip were not worth any discussion about my health or wellbeing.

Of course, I was even more isolated and suffered ongoing abuse in California. A slow fire burned inside me. I was angry and devastated that our son was growing up in a dynamic of violence, hypocrisy, and fear.

Even as a little baby who had only begun to walk, Caleb occasionally came towards me and laid his head on my lap when the screaming, stand over tactics, and intimidation started. Those moments were breathtaking and eye opening. Children perceive all. Their spirits know even when they are unable to express or articulate what they feel. In the car where the rages often happened, I would look back at the car seat and see terror on our baby's little face. My begging and pleading— *"Please don't do this with Caleb in the car"*—amounted to nothing.

The truth about abuse is that it is an ongoing cycle of violence with three main cogs turning the wheel: blame, denial, and minimization. He was always right. I was always wrong. Lies, deceit, domination, betrayals, and punishments became a way of life.

I did not leave to protect myself. I had disintegrated to zero. However, the commitment I had to Caleb was totally intact, and I knew in my heart that this life was unacceptable for him to endure. With the help of Enrique's relatives, who had witnessed the violence and abuse, I was able to escape. Even though they turned against me later, they helped at the time, and I do not think I could have escaped without them.

A cause of immeasurable sadness was that there were pastors in America and Australia who supported Caleb's father. They helped him and they had 'grace' for him. It is crucial to understand that the way to help an abuser is through accountability and not grace. Grace will be exploited by people who operate without conscience. The pastors who assisted Enrique allowed him free rein to continue his abuse. He followed us to Australia four months after we escaped, with a strong intention of continuing to attack me. He was enabled by people I thought would help and protect me. The pain and betrayal I felt was all consuming.

In his mind, it was time to punish me for leaving him. "You're going down. I will take you down. I will wait, as long as I have to, and you will go down." Those were the words of his chilling, threatening phone call when he arrived in Australia.

The idea of submission is fraught in some religious communities. It is drilled into abused women that they must submit to all kinds of vile treatment in the name of God. This is surely anathema in a Christian context? Enrique had strong beliefs that women should not be educated or take on any form of leadership.

The marriage bed and the church are meant to be the safest places on earth. For many, they are the most painful, dangerous, and damaging.

The proactive steps I took to heal from these deeply traumatic years depended on me being able to feel gratitude and move beyond being a victim.

"Healing begins when you shed the victim mentality."

~ Linda

I struggled to find ways to be grateful. I felt that darkness was surrounding me. Living in survival mode made it almost impossible to feel, emote, or connect my emotions to events. All was suppressed in the name of survival.

To compound my already overwhelming grief and heartache, I began to receive multiple harsh and condemning letters from members of the congregation of the church in California, who saw Enrique only as godly. They were explaining that I had failed to submit to my husband because I had left him. I must return. Not one of them asked why I left, if I was okay, or if they could help in any way. A truly disturbing response. The instant assumption that I was "wrong" was awfully concerning, and I recall being stunned and hurt. I had a constant inability to process what was happening, how this was possible, and how no one seemed to stop him. He had the community of the church and the pastors fooled.

I experienced an enormous amount of spiritual abuse, not only in the marriage, but from these leaders, pastors, and church members who threw layers of blame and shame upon me, all in the name of Jesus. Using the Bible as a weapon to abuse and hurt, Scripture twisting, and toxic religion wrapped in legalism is a deadly combination.

"Search your heart, and recognize your sin."

"Did you leave to force his hand? You need to cling to your husband for richer or for poorer and be subject to your husband. He faithfully comes to church, but something is amiss: You are not there. He is the head of the house."

"Ask for forgiveness from God."

"You don't want to honor Christ!!"

I am completely convinced that God abhors spiritual abuse and the domestic violence that underpins it.

Fortunately, our Japanese pastor in Nagano saw right through the façade: *"I witnessed personally and was aware of Enrique's continual abusive behaviour towards Simone. It included humiliation, verbal abuse, hateful language, and threats."*

I was so grateful to this enlightened man. I was also overwhelmed with gratitude when I found a wonderful counsellor who walked me through the process, through which I was able to divorce my persecutor. What a joyful and freeing day it was!

"Freedom is the oxygen of the soul." ~ Moshe Dayan

I had still tried to 'turn the other cheek' after I escaped, yet the attacks did not relent. One day I read this verse in a brand new light.

It spoke straight to my spirit after years of brainwashing:

"God has called us to live in peace." ~ 1 Corinthians 7:15b

Well it cannot be both, I thought. I am either called to abuse or peace. One or the other. Life with him is abuse, which apparently is NOT my calling, so I can choose peace.

This sounds so obvious and basic, yet psychological abuse can truly destroy and deceive our thinking.

In 2006, three years after I left, Enrique was arrested and charged for the sexual assaults against me. This crime carried a fourteen-year jail term if he was found guilty.

His bail conditions prohibited him from coming within one hundred meters of me and required him to surrender his passport and report to the police station twice a week.

While testifying in criminal court about his abuse, I froze and went blank when giving evidence. This was a major letdown for the prosecution. My usual ability to be somewhat articulate was conquered by a mixture of the trauma of reliving so much horror, the continual court cases, and a belligerent defense barrister bombarding me—a barrister trained to go in for the kill and determined to discredit every word I said.

According to the law, Enrique's punishment was meant to be much more severe.

The police who had arrested him were dismayed at the result and said, "The whole room knows he is guilty. Unfortunately, this is how the law works."

I was devastated. He seemed to "get away" with everything he did.

My victim support person, Rose, who was assigned by the court, was lovely. Rose and the police encouraged me to apply for a new case as a victim of crime.

In two separate cases in the New South Wales Victims of Crime Tribunal, I received compensation in 2010 for category three sexual assault—the highest category. A year prior to that I had also received category three domestic violence compensation and the perpetrator of these crimes was my former husband—a missionary. They were not large amounts, as they were government compensation grants, yet finally I began to feel some validation.

I was so grateful that the crimes were acknowledged, at least by the Tribunal. Sadly, the money received was reinvested into the legal costs that arose from the separation.

I was free from the marriage, yet not free of him. The most dangerous time is said to be when a woman leaves an abuser, and it is common knowledge that if they cannot reach you anymore, they will often target your children. That is exactly what happened. Years of trauma and lies ensued, and my son Caleb and I walked a very difficult and challenging road.

I made healing and moving forward my absolute mission. My finances were devastated, my health was destroyed, and my heart was broken. I had PTSD and horrible flashbacks of past events. Who I was and who I desired to be were incongruent, and restoration was my only hope.

I became devoted to studying, training, reading, learning, growing, emoting, praying, fasting, singing, writing, fitness, working, courses, counselling, and health.

Over, and over, and over, I did everything I could possibly do to clear trauma, align with my true self, and heal. I grieved deeper than I can explain; no words will ever suffice.

I worked at it like a full-time job on top of everything else I did. This was a battle I had to overcome. For me, for my son, and for anyone on this road.

"Now if you know what you're worth, then go out and get what you're worth."

– Rocky Balboa

I had generous, loving parents and incredible friends who cheered me on every step of the way, unwavering in their support year in, year out. My best friend Rachelle even gave me her car, which is a moment in time I will never forget.

Through the heartache, I intentionally became increasingly fearless, clear, knowledgeable, and focused.

I became the strongest person I knew.

Through the unresolved grief, I wrote inspirational songs and trained my soul with diligence to respond to everything from a victorious place rather than be a victim. It is tender and beautiful work to free the soul. It is holy, sacred, and hard. It is extremely challenging to escape such brutality, and with everyone's help—I did.

I say it is happening FOR me not TO me. My dear friend Melanie Tonia Evans, who is a narcissistic abuse recovery expert, taught me about the gift in abuse. Often, these perpetrators are AIDs (angels in disguise) who allow us to truly find ourselves, so that we can detach once and for all and evolve into a life of thriving.

Before I was married, I studied at Berklee College of Music in Boston on a scholarship. I completed my degree, a *Bachelor of Arts in Contemporary Music,* and won the Nescafe Big Break worth $20,000.

For years whilst I was married, I hardly ever sang. Every part of me was diminished and controlled, and I was rendered voiceless.

After I left, and as I began to heal, I started to sing again. I toured with top artists like the Grammy-award-winning Taylor Dayne and Max Pellicano. I was mentored by one of the most respected singers in Australia, Kerrie Biddell. Kerrie taught me about life as much as she taught me about music, and her support was powerful through all the difficult years.

I performed multiple times in Parliament House for national leaders. I graduated with my Master of Music Degree from the Sydney Conservatorium of Music with a High Distinction for Jazz Vocal and presented my research at Auckland University. I recorded a jazz album, *My Romance,* and an album of my original music, Surrender, with incredible Australian musicians, and launched the records to sold-out audiences in top Sydney live music venues. I made multiple music videos and recorded an EP, *New Day,* with an American faith-based record label to assist bringing freedom and awareness for those trapped in sex trafficking. I am now an ambassador for this cause.

When I think of the richness of the lyrics in so many of my songs that were birthed during intense periods, this quote comes to mind.

"Thank you for the tragedy. I need it for my art." ~ Kurt Cobain

I lived in permanent hope and faith in God that I would feel freedom and peace in my heart. I deliberately remained grateful and found ways to reside in a place of gratitude. I am even grateful for the crushing, because through it all, I was able to heal generational issues, weak/non-existent boundaries, and false beliefs. I found disowned, orphaned, fragmented, and wounded parts of my soul and brought them together for healing.

Gratitude is one of the strongest weapons in my arsenal. There were many times that were extremely bleak, where I would struggle to find ANYTHING to be grateful for, and I would force myself to find something.

"I am grateful I can see the sun on that leaf."

"I am grateful I have water to drink."

"I am grateful I can breathe."

"I am grateful to have such loving parents and friends."

The basics.

"Gratitude is our ability to see the grace of God, morning by morning, no matter what else greets us in the course of the day."

~ Craig Barnes

That is where I started and where I reverted to whenever needed. The more gratitude I employed, the more I was able to overcome. The more I was thankful, the more I began to master my emotions and radically take full responsibility for everything in my life. There are no mistakes, there is always a higher purpose, and nothing is impossible with God.

I worked hard to reignite a new way of being that was GRATEFUL. It took discipline, perseverance, and persistence, and I never gave up. Unconditional love for myself during the whole process was paramount.

I have learned how to release what hinders me and "keep my peace on" by cultivating an attitude of gratitude in all things.

I discovered there is no pit too deep, no chain too strong, and there is no pain or heartache that cannot be overcome.

With a heart full of gratitude, I can honestly say that I truly see the richness all around me as a result of this extremely difficult road. I have met amazing people who show their resilience and strength as they pursue justice, and I have had wonderful opportunities as a result of doing the inner work to heal.

I encourage you to LISTEN to your intuition. Listen to your heart song. Do what makes your heart sing. Live the Song of Your Life!

**"You can cage the singer
but not the song."**

~ Harry Belafonte

You can trust you. You can trust God. I did not trust me. I said yes when my heart said no. I did not have my own back. I did not even know how to. Pleasing others at your own expense is not just silly, it is dangerous.

The lifeline you have been given is the MUSIC that is unique to you. Your music that comes from your own soul. Attune to that, hear that, and sing that every day through your highest beliefs, thoughts, words, and actions. The alignment you create will save your life, bring you abundant peace, and make you unstoppable.

Always remember:

"You have a voice, you were born to live in freedom, to feel comfortable in your skin, and to know what victory feels like. You were born to win." – Simone Waddell

_____

_____

*Caleb and Enrique are pseudonyms.

**"The more you praise and
celebrate your life,
the more there is in life to
celebrate."**

~ Oprah Winfrey

CHAPTER FIVE

Infinite Gratitude for Eternal Love

By King Gabriel Quincy Collymore

To speak of gratitude from a strictly physical and earthly perspective would be, in My opinion, to do the World and Myself a tremendous injustice.

From My point of view and discovery, the world is much more than a physical display, hologram, or program of any sort. It is a Living, expanding idea that is forever evolving and growing to greater levels of expression and experience. However, in My opinion, it is only by a conscious choice to share Love in a deliberate beautification and improvement process that the innate value and miraculous nature of this experience can be even remotely captured by the senses.

Think not that this is an attempt to nullify or in any way diminish the beauty that exists within Life experience. In My opinion, it is an honest look at what I know reality to be, and a choice to have its vision, and the attitudes derived therein, be of importance to Me. My acceptance of it allows it to be accessible to Others, and this has been aided by My choice to act in accordance with its structure and content.

This perspective may appear to be a delusion to many who may rely totally on provided data and systemic disinformation to verify truth. Nonetheless, I have come to discover that not only is the truth not found in the world, but also, it can only be found within

One's Self, as has been said by Sages, Mystics and Wise Women through the ages.

It's quite often said that spiritual growth is most often spurred on by great tragedy or suffering. Yet, the experience and interpretation of such events are dependent on the Individual experiencing such adversity, and His/Her perspective at that point in time.

That being said, I can genuinely say that the fluctuations in My perspective throughout this experience have afforded Me many opportunities to choose, again and again, what was actually of importance to Myself and those for whom I declared My care and admiration.

Here, then, is an honest and somewhat randomly constructed account of the moments in Life that have stood out to Me as memorable and formative, which have led to a sense of gratitude for Life which is beyond what I would have been capable of experiencing in any other set of circumstances. It is the foundation of My experience. They may appear to be random because this is the way My mind functions, and the ability to lay it out as it is for You to get an intimate view, as well as an uninhibited feel of the inner workings of this mind, fills me with a sense of peace.

These moments are also the underpinnings of the world I presently see and enjoy. Yet, I know that they, too, are choices and will continue to be adjusted and rewritten, as Life offers endless opportunities for change. May they offer You insight into the reason for the deep sense of gratitude that I now have, for all that I have and am.

I was a very quiet child who had an affinity for dirt snacks (allegedly rolling up the front carpet to pour huge quantities into My mouth to have a crunchy munch). As time progressed, My other hobbies came to include pet ants, lizards, and lighting fires with magnifying glasses.

I was very dependent on my relationship with My Mother. I had moments of gazing at trees for hours in the backyard, which would reflect and resonate a sense of quietude akin to a space that I was oddly familiar with.

I hardly ever spoke in My early days, according to My parents' accounts and My own recollection. This was mainly because I was very involved in observing and felt less inclined to share My observations. In other words, I was allowing Myself to come to a more complete view of the inner workings of this experience.

I cried on the first day of Kindergarten, on My Mother's rapid departure from the lightly grilled front gate of Happy Vale Montessori, which had a name that quite accurately described the atmosphere. Though I was greeted by smiling and reassuring faces, none seemed to quell the deep dependency and attachment that I felt for My Mother; with a sense of foreboding, I looked out the front gate, dressed in My checkered turquoise and white shirt and short khaki pants. As if to prove My psychic prediction right, My Mother vanished in a Houdini-like fashion, as I cannot even recall seeing her walk away. Maybe it was a crafty act of misdirection performed by My new and welcoming Companions.

This was the first time, being away from the comfort of My Mother's company, and that of Our little house in the tranquil village of River Estate, Diego Martin, a town known for cocoa production and a historical water wheel, which had a quality of almost magical appeal.

I found out quite a bit later that My Mother had lived in this tropical haven with Her Family for a while before They decided to ship off to the Americas to gain a better livelihood.

My Dad seemed, for the first four years of My Life, to be more of a Visitor than a steady figure and was welcomed to Our house with estranged and questioning looks from My curious and possessive childhood mind.

I later discovered that this scarcity of His presence was due to the disharmony in familial relation, explained generously by My Grandmother. She upheld a firm biblical adherence and required proper behavioral etiquette for Everyone—except for Herself, as there were many unexplained differences in the complexions of Her Kids, Their last names, and Their general appearance.

There was also a need there, for Her to ensure that Everyone "praised the Lord" with every breath of Their waking hours, and this was done rather vociferously in the resonance of the ceramic-tiled front gallery, which had the acoustic characteristics of a Roman Catholic Cathedral; in this way, the neighbors could hear and join into the chorus of praise to The Highest as well.

In Her presence, there was no space for "idle minds" like Mine to wander or wonder, as all the answers were undoubtedly available in the most excellent book, as interpreted by the great and worshipful minds of that era. (Just in case You missed it, I'm being a little sarcastic.)

An occasional solid whooping would ensure that I didn't forget to offer My daily/hourly praise to the Creator of all this glorious knowledge that was a wellspring of great Joy in judging the wrongs and rights of Human function, interaction and thinking.

I was deemed the "Devil Child," for reasons I may never fully comprehend. As far as I can tell, it seemed to be due to my inability to dogmatically accept thoughts that made absolutely no sense and mostly inhibited the pure freedom of My curiosity and exploration of My environment.

I was physically strong, with huge powerful calves and a somewhat stocky physique, which earned Me a few nicknames that I inwardly rejected, but reluctantly condoned, as it was the custom in My place of birth. These were names such as Zeus, Hercules, and a few others that were far too facetious to mention. I found Myself partaking in many competitive sports, including swimming, track and field, and soccer (then referred to as football), which contributed to my distinct physique.

I was successful athletically and academically inclined, as was the mandate laid down by My Parents; however, I was somewhat laid-back in My approach to studies. This was displayed very differently than Most would expect, as I would rush to get My work done immediately if possible, just so that I could have time to relax and be unburdened from the thoughts and pressure of having to get schoolwork done. I appeared to be a good student, masking the fact that I had so many other interests and desires that spoke to Me in the depths of My Being. I really just wanted the distractions of schoolwork out of the way.

I obtained a score on the Scholastic Assessment Test (SAT) that allowed Me entry on a full Scholarship to Morgan State University (a Historically Black University), which was revered for its Electrical Engineering and Music Programs. At Morgan State, My innate interests arose once again. While burying Myself in Engineering material in hopes of financial success, I was drawn toward music as if it was the breath of Life itself. It came to Me as songs, melodies and fully developed performances in My dreams and waking fantasies.

One day, while sprint-walking My way back from the music building, My eyes landed upon a radiantly beautiful smile, velvety smooth chocolate skin, and a confidently playful demeanor. I connected with a twinkle in Her eye, said hi, and within a few weeks, She was my Girlfriend. I became very attached to Her, a fact I was unaware of until it was time to detach.

We were together for two years and then came the challenge.

I was very lenient and understanding of a very "friendly" relationship with a teammate of Hers; in hindsight, maybe a bit too accommodating.

She certainly aided Me in realizing My fears, and We had a pretty bad break up. And by "pretty bad," I mean crying like I did on My first day of school (only this time in My bedroom, thinking I would die because My heart felt like it was going to burst.)

No amount of rational thinking was helpful at that time; nonetheless I kept telling Myself that one day I would be able to look back on it and laugh. I had an extremely difficult time believing that thought at the time, though.

In that period of utter despair and grief, I began to sing all the songs that I Loved and had been singing and writing that much more fervently. I poured Myself into the lyrics, melodies, and emotion as if I had written these sorrowful mantras of heartbreaks and lost Love Myself.

By listening to Stevie Wonder, Nat King Cole, Glen Lewis, and Carl Thomas religiously, I developed a finely tuned ear and a voice that could very closely mimic quite a few of the classics.

I also found Myself through My passion and hunger to deepen this connection, as I was being taught by classical music teachers three times a week during My lunch hour. I found that the music had triggered a great movement of energy within what I now know to be My hara region, but at that time referred to as My gut.

It felt like a contact with a brand new spiritual force within Me.

I experienced an intense desire to sing My heart out and communicate in a way that allowed Me to express this depth of emotion that I had experienced. It seemed as if the mysteries of this Life that I had been engrossed in since childhood were now revealing themselves to Me, though not in a language that I perceived Myself as being fully fluent in just yet.

I very much wanted to relate this feeling to Others, as I knew this was a part of My Life's plan that seemed to have been with Me from the days of childhood tree gazing and fantasizing.

Despite this deep draw, I didn't pursue a career in pop music, though I created quite a wonderful and enjoyable repertoire (in the form of three published CDs).

I then began a deepening of My meditation efforts and began to have glimpses of what was coming into My Life experience.

I had a vision of Myself singing on a large stage, wearing a golden dashiki, and clearly knew that this would happen two years later.

And indeed, two years later, as if by clockwork, there I was singing on stage, in a golden dashiki, at the Agape International Spiritual Center in Los Angeles, California, and was very much into my further Spiritual development.

This was a part of Life that I had always focused on within but had never really made a topic of conversation or expression, as I was aware that there was no space for My radical views in the environments in which I lived.

You see, I first became aware of Myself as existing in a dimension of light and space, and in this dimension, there was Another that was exactly as I was, made of the most radiant golden-white light. We had eyes of pure and brilliant quality, but no mouths, as there was no need for them because We communicated in a way that I can only describe as an instantaneous knowing. It wasn't a transference of thought, as in telepathy, but more of quantum communication with simultaneous observation. In today's scientific terminology, this could be referred to as a type of quantum entanglement of minds.

In this space, with this Other, I became aware of how deeply the Other was at rest, yet I was interested in the geometrical shape of the space and began to explore its makeup. I then looked past what seemed to be an edge or transparent wall and saw something that looked different from what I had already known and experienced. It appeared to be a solid substance, and by paying attention to it, I began to feel different from the Other for the first time.

I began to feel a vibration that emanated from My body of light, and there, this physical journey began.

Born on a stormy night in Trinidad and Tobago, My journey toward expressing what I came to be began. I was met with a Family of very eclectic interests, including athletics, academics, religion, and spirituality. Naturally, I became interested in exploring the workings and functions of this new dimension. I was intrigued by Life and genuinely curious about exactly what it was. Yet, it was only by a thorough investigation of its creatures and organisms that I could get a deeper understanding of what I was actually experiencing.

Through a natural inclination to remain in touch with the vibration of peace in which I previously existed; I became a Meditator without any idea that that was what I was doing. This happened as a result of the fact that at that time, there was no electricity in the house in which I lived, and We lit kerosene lamps at night. On staring into the lamp's entrancing and captivating flame, I came to develop a focused relaxation that allowed Me to really sense the fullness and quality of the space surrounding and within everything.

I sensed a quality about this space that I could not quite describe comparatively, yet I felt it in a profoundly deep and tangible way.

The thought rose in My mind, that I would have a positive effect on the world and that it would involve sharing the feelings, ideas, and experiences I had. I also sensed that music would be involved and would deepen My relationship with these topics and the beautiful Souls that I encountered through My depth of receptivity. A product of this impetus is a song I wrote and produced by the name of "Everything I see," available for listening on iTunes, Amazon.link drop, and YouTube (https://www.youtube.com/watch?v=hkebpslolJA)

This was My personal experience of this energy, as I was musically inclined; yet Others Who have walked a path that is similar have shared Their perspectives, attitudes, and analysis of It through Poetry, e.g., the Sufi poet Rumi; acts that defy the known limits of the body's capabilities, e.g., Wim Hoff, "The Iceman," along with some of the Tibetan Monks; enlightening discourse and lectures, e.g., Neville Goddard, a Caribbean Mystic and Author and Explorer; and many Others in various artistic and communicative expressions. What They all have in common is that

They have gotten a glimpse of the Presence that resides within Us All.

So back to My multi-temporaneous view of My Life's unfolding...

By the age of seven, through a focus on the third eye space (the area just above the middle of the eyebrows), I realized that there was no such thing as 'nothing.' This came through the observation that when I focused on the third eye's space and contemplated what appeared there, I noticed a blank, void-like, black space there. Yet, as I attempted to remove the black void with My thoughts, a white void became present, and on trying to remove the white void, a black void appeared again, and on and on this went.

I accepted that regardless of what was removed, there would always be something that replaced the last image. I became aware that the perception itself was generated by the existence of something. I then saw that in order to observe anything, You must do so with something. Therefore, the starting point of analysis was already somewhat faulty, as "something" must be in relationship with "something else" for the idea of perception to even arise; therefore, there are already at least two things from the beginning. Simply, the concept of nothing was already "something;" hence there was, in reality, no such thing as nothing. I grew in understanding My journey toward the expression of Myself, and I was able to access a degree of experiential verification for what Life was showing to and through Me. This came from the practice of Astral Travel (a.k.a. Out-of-Body Experiences), Dreamwork, Deliberate Intention, Spiritual Practices, and regular meditation.

At age ten, due to the Sunday School trips to an Anglican/Christian church in My neighborhood, which willingly taught Us all about the "Jesus" shaped hole that all humans had, which could be filled by no other than Jesus Christ, I had a very traumatic dream, in which the earth was crumbling, and "Jesus" (the European version) appeared on a bus from the sky, and took Me on board a boat. From the front of this boat, I could see the earth crumbling, and My Mother was on the shore. I stood in the presence of this Jesus and said to My Mother, "I will never leave You." That was My promise, and then I awoke. Unknown to Me at that time, this promise would later be the foundation of a new Life.

It became quite clear to Me that there was much more discovery to be done, so My first significant eye-opening experience was a meditation I was prompted to do, of My own volition.

This is quite literally what I did:

> ➢ I relaxed from toe to head.

> ➢ I focused on breathing naturally while placing attention on the area of the physical heart.

> ➢ I became aware of all the changes that were taking place, but passively.

> ➢ I did not attempt to change or fiddle with the energy that was presented. I just observed it and appreciated it.

As simple as that sounds, the effects were mind-blowing, and created a new space within Me that I was previously unaware of. I have run thousands of Others through this very simple process with astounding results, ranging from visions and clairaudient experiences, to full-on liberation experiences (Nirvana/Satori/Samadhi).

I mean, light shows such as I had never seen before, electromagnetic and electric pulses, and visions of the makeup of the inner world were a sort of manual that I could learn from in a welcoming, self-study environment.

This was followed by an event in which I had one of My first successful astral projections, and the first thing that came to My mind was to go to the mirror in My room, to see what the form of body I was in. To My surprise and amusement, I saw a silhouette; not empty, but totally filled with what I interpreted to be stars, galaxies, and a universe. I then named My musical CD, which I was releasing at that time, "The Realization of Infiniti," spelled with an I instead of a Y, to suggest that I was the eternal aspect of the Universe itself, made visible and tangible. I was both excited and inspired by this experience, because while I had been taught that there was a void, I had discovered that there was no such thing.

There was an entire Universe within Me. This was just a precursor of things to come and experiences to be had. I would have gladly shared, yet those experiences are so vast and extensive, that they deserve their own space, time, and domain. In applying what Life has given me, I have discovered a few things that really allowed Me to be grateful, not only for what I have, but for what I am.

Through My experience with the many beautiful energies of Life experience, I have come to see Life, and the power that fosters, sustains, and maintains it as precious, beyond comparison and reason. I would refer to it as the offspring of Fulfillment and Bliss, which brings Me to another experience that came about both unexpectedly and sanctioned. I had been practicing a specific technique that was given to Me via a download due to the frequency I was occupying at that time. The instruction was to be aware of a particular vibration in all My thoughts and actions. I performed this conditioning of the mind regularly. On this particular day in September 2009, I was pulled to have a "sit down" (meditation), and as soon as I sat, everything disappeared, and by everything, I mean everything that I could point to or refer to as the world I had known.

All that remained was a sense of being, followed by liquid light of a golden-white hue. This light was Me, yet simultaneously, I could view it from the outside. It was a sort of total inner-outer, full-spectrum, all-angled vision. I felt My awareness focused on a specific region of the expression. All that was felt was perfect fulfillment, which I later referred to as Fulfillment/Bliss, as that encompassed what I was feeling in My seemingly inadequate vocabulary of the body's sensations. The thing about this Joy was that there was no reason whatsoever for it. It was all-permeating, all-pervading, and all there was.

There was a greater Joy felt by knowing that it could not be taken away, as there was no reason for it to be there and therefore, nothing that could cause it to go by any change or loss. I knew that I had it, and it was all that I would ever need.

I remained in this state for an indefinite period, and then, I had a flashback to the promise I had made to My Mother at the age of ten.

I had said that I would never leave without Her. As that thought came to My awareness, there I was in a body again, filled with Joy, and yet also with a sense of remorse for returning to the world. However, even this was conflicted, as I knew that I had a purpose. That purpose entailed being that point of memory of Life beyond Life, firstly for My beloved Mother, but also for all Others who had walked a similar or aligned path and Who were looking for a different perspective on Life.

As I said at the beginning, to speak of gratitude merely from a physical perspective would be to do the world and Myself a great injustice, and I do firmly believe that We are all One, so it couldn't be any Other way. I urge you as the Reader of this account of My journey up to this point, to explore, dare to inquire, find what is really there, because once You know it's there, You cannot help but be abundantly grateful for Life, Love, and All that is.

Thank You Divine Spirit for joining Me in this story of The Life that I have Lived, and please take what You may from it. May it in some way make Your Life experience brighter, more hopeful, and more meaningful. After all, You are Life Itself, My Beloved Friend.

I am forever grateful.

Eternal Love and Infinite Peace.

"The more that we feel grateful in our lives, the more joy and fulfillment we're able to feel."

~ Miranda Anderson

CHAPTER SIX

Grace and Guidance

By Elizabeth Ross-Boag

I often sit with a warm cup of peppermint tea, freshly picked from the garden, and contemplate what life would be like if I could not live in gratitude. The value of gratitude has been a close companion throughout my entire life. Especially amongst all the adversity, turmoil, and tests that I've had to endure during this journey that we call life. I've always felt a sense of gratitude because of the natural, sacred, and heartfelt connection I have with the creator and the universe. The peace I feel from regularly being mindful of gratitude brings me deep daily reflections and a natural sense of the creator's lessons.

> **"Gratitude makes sense of the past, brings**
> **peace for today,**
> **and creates a vision for tomorrow."**

~ Melody Beattie

As one who desires to be a child of God, I perceive my application to life as a yearning for daily inspiring association that reminds me of our blessings. Attitude is so vitally important. The right attitude of gratitude and open-mindedness has the power to change everything.

Have you heard of Bhakti yoga? Bhakti means devotion and yoga means to connect, so Bhakti yoga is the process of connecting to divinity through the practice of devotion. My greatest essence of gratitude has been the blessings given to me from practicing Bhakti

Yoga. Bhakti Yoga is the highest limb of yoga, which is ultimately living a life enriched with a mood of devotional service to the divine, a scientific process towards self-realization. I have graciously been blessed with this process of yoga for over two decades.

As in my previous chapter in the *A Journey of Riches edition, In Search of Happiness*, I outline my life journey of facing adversity while learning to become equipoised, unaffected, and ultimately content. How can someone maintain their cool after being struck with such a heavy load of tests and adversity? And still be content with life? Well a secret in the path of Bhakti Yoga is to take the humble position. The benefits of applying a sweet, serving mood in life are limitless. This actually means to realize that all the challenges that come to test us are ultimately blessings in disguise. The loving hand of the Lord comes to help us find out more about our true selves. Remembering that the divine is within our very heart has the potential to change our perspective on life and the way we cope with day-to-day situations. Giving rise to a more wholesome vision helps to shift our awareness to access the bigger picture.

However, I must say, this process that I am practicing would not be possible without the grace and guidance of my spiritual master's magnanimous example. His ever-flowing abundant example of kindness and love towards all who come into his presence has completely saved me from the trappings of grief and depression so common in this present day and age. My spiritual teacher's name is Bhakti Sundar Govinda Maharaj. I am so grateful for His guidance and teachings that my only desire is to dedicate my whole life to sharing the benefits of His teachings with others. He has provided me with so much nectar, shelter, and protection that I have been able to cope with all the adversities that I was trapped in for so long. His teachings provide me with the tools to free myself from bad habits and conditioned patterns that seemed to add to my suffering. To this day, I truly feel I am unaffected by those tests because of His sweet grace and mercy.

"In return for my insignificant surrender, You have mercifully bestowed upon me, Your servant, the torchlight of transcendental knowledge. Therefore, what devotee of Yours who has any gratitude could ever give up Your lotus feet and take shelter of another master?" SB 11.29.38

His Divine Grace Srila Bhakti Sundar Govinda Maharaj departed from this world on March 27, 2010. To stay connected to Him, I had to align my lifestyle with His teachings in every possible way. By following His teachings, I have remained in His association to this day. Although it is not easy, Bhakti won't enter your heart just by saying the word *Bhakti*. You have to apply yourself in various ways, such as rising at 4:30 a.m. daily. Bhakti yoga provides me with an ocean of inspiration and close connection to a community of supportive associations that reminds me to be grateful 24/7. The main teaching—to practice humility, tolerance, and giving honor to others without desiring it for yourself—has helped to open my heart in ways I had never thought possible.

It is also imperative on this path to get in the association of Bhaktas (practitioners) that are superior to us and that have the mood and understanding that we want. In the last two years, I have been blessed with this supportive and inspiring association, which in Sanskrit is called *Sadhu Sangha* (association of saintly persons). In the last two years, I have visited our central temple in Nabadwip, West Bengal, India. A good supportive association is 99.9% of the process. As a direct result of receiving a good association at Nabadwip, I have been deeply fixed in a state of consciousness that is peaceful and happy. These saintly characters genuinely lead by example and are sincerely good-hearted, kind, and inspiring to be around. The care that they provide is so genuine and like no other that I have witnessed in my life before. These sincere sadhus (saints) happily encourage me daily to practice from the heart, not the head, and they unconditionally check in on my personal progress towards self-realization.

When taking the time to reflect on one's life and recognizing that it's such a big journey, it's important to be mindful and reflect upon your daily progress. Self-analysis has helped me to realize that every day I wake up is another excellent opportunity, a precious gift. When you can be honest and look ahead and behind on the path you've been walking, you will see that there have been many blessings in disguise, many tests and challenges that have helped develop your character. Somehow you are now actually grateful for those moments of difficulty.

"Feeling gratitude and not expressing it is like wrapping a present and not giving it."

~ William Arthur Ward

I've had a life filled with challenges and adversity, but I know that all of the pain, all of the suffering and the tests I have faced have truly defined who I am today. I am happy with who I have transformed to become. In all honesty, my greatest fortune is being blessed with the guidance, teachings, and spiritual community that my spiritual master provided to help me desire to be a good-hearted person.

I realize now on my life's journey that I was very fortunate to be born into such a big family. I am the youngest of ten, with three fathers and a mother who worked so very hard. All of those trials and tribulations while growing up nudged me in the direction of the biggest blessing of my life: taking shelter in a genuine spiritual master. He was always calling me home, guiding me through the chaos. I look back at all of the horrors and painful memories of my childhood and realize that I was always protected and sheltered from being exposed to the full depths of the horror by his grace and mercy, his constant guardianship.

Later I will reveal how this realization came to be. As the youngest of ten, my kind and caring nature always came into play when my siblings or other intimate family members needed an unbiased approach to alter some conflicting circumstances. Quite often, my approach to mediation would harmonize the conflicting issue or drama.

Throughout my entire childhood, I was fortunate to have a strong connection with God and chose to be part of a Christian mission that provided many retreats, services, and camps catered to young people. This fed me an overwhelming abundant flow of gratitude, as I was always seeking Christian fellowship. I was allowed to be an influential leader amongst our Christian mission and community. I developed leadership skills during these camps and retreats and would confidently coordinate workshops and group activities, encouraging fellow members to engage deeply by sharing their experiences and their fellowship. A connection to the divine and the desire to share that experience with others has always been the saving grace in my life.

The turmoil of a dysfunctional family life continued through my teens with my elder sibling's catastrophic decisions that seemed to affect all of us in the family. However, the mercy was pouring into my life more than ever. At this period of my life, I was introduced to powerful and influential role models that provided ongoing support and shelter. My closest girlfriend from primary school, Shaz, and her family, the Goughs, rescued me every time an emergency surfaced, sheltering me when I had to stay away from home as a matter of life or death. The Goughs were, in my eyes, the ideal family. They gave me endless compassion and made me feel welcome, especially if I needed shelter on a school day. They always knew how to make everything okay and normal for me, even amidst the chaos. They would give me enough love and support to fuel my attitude of gratitude in knowing that at least they cared for me.

And then there's the story of my first high school boyfriend. Unbelievably, he is the founder of the *A Journey of Riches* series, our dear John Spender himself. You see, our relationship was so pure and innocent, from the start to now. Back then, I did not view him as my high school boyfriend. I viewed him as a soul mate and teacher. He taught me so much in these trying years as a teenager, generally by being a good person, dedicated to clean living and an active lifestyle. I used to watch him walk across the quadrangle of my high school and would feel so grateful to know him. He protected me in a schoolyard of over 1000 students. Even when we chose to go our separate ways and the relationship ended, he always looked out for me. And now, in 2020, twenty-seven years later, our friendship has developed so that we remain very close spiritually. This brings me deep gratitude to realize—"Good friends are like the stars. We may not see them all the time, but we always know they are there." (Christy Evans)

Not long after that romance ended, I met my second lover, Murari, and quickly started a family. He was not only my lover but my god brother. During that time of developing marriage and family, I was a dedicated yoga student, studying to be a personal trainer and yoga teacher. This is where my real life began. I was awakened to simple living and high thinking.

At 18, I gave birth to my first child, Keziah Sundar, and I was then introduced to the Krishna Consciousness movement, made up of devotees who worship Lord Krishna and practice Bhakti yoga. At that time, at such a young age, I was blessed with meeting my spiritual teacher, and he captured my heart the instant I met him.

Leading to that first meeting, Murari and I had been on our honeymoon with our firstborn, 18-month-old son Keziah. We were staying at a Christian community house in Bangalow, inland from Byron Bay, Australia. The Byron Bay region is renowned for its entertaining market life. We were at a Sunday market when we met some of our spiritual master's disciples for the first time. These disciples fed us the most sumptuous vegetarian feast and chanted with us in the market ground hall. We felt so blessed that they embraced us beautifully, and we were extremely grateful for the delicious food they fed us. They also invited us to their ashram for a festival during the coming week. Things were not going very well back at the Christian community house. The managers were becoming extraordinarily possessive and controlling. So we decided to move on. "Where will we go?" I asked my husband. "Let's head out to the mountains to find those beautiful people we met at the markets on Sunday," he said. And that's exactly what we did.

We winded through the Tweed Valley and pulled up to the ashram under Mount Warning in Uki, New South Wales, Australia, where the sweet disciples had invited us. One of our spiritual masters' best friends, Siddhanti Maharaj, was there waiting at the gate for us and asked if we were the family from Bangalow. We replied, "Yes, we are." He answered, "Come with me. My Gurudev (beloved spiritual master) has been waiting for you to arrive." We were amazed that they were aware of our arrival.

My son was 18 months old and his personality was to observe before getting to know a new person. He was generally timid. As soon as he saw my spiritual master, however, he ran through a crowd of over 100 students straight up to him. This 18-month-old boy bowed to the feet of our soon-to-be Gurudev and then climbed up onto his lap. They were both laughing with so much joy. My Gurudev said, "Oh, my boy, I have been waiting for you for so long."

I witnessed a full past-life relationship reconnecting and had to surrender and trust that my son was safe in this stranger's lap. This stranger was soon to become my spiritual master.

Soon after being introduced to our spiritual master, Srila Govinda Maharaj, I was given a new name, Indumati, meaning the Heart of the Moon. A few days afterward, my 18-month-old son walked into my spiritual master's room and said, "Gurudev, why my mum and dad got a new name? I want a new name too!" My master laughed with ecstatic joy and said, "This is wonderful!" He then sat my son at his feet and named him Krishna Sundar, speaking the meaning: the Beautiful Son of the All-beautiful. Their connection with each other was immediate. I have never witnessed a connection like this before.

Srila Govinda Maharaj showed me by His exemplary example, the path of humility, respect, and tolerance in every aspect of life and taught me so much about myself that I had never known before. His ability to give unconditional love to all who came before him has given me a deep awareness of my own true self. It has helped create the insight to accept my abilities and be grateful for every precious moment.

For everyone dies, but not everyone truly lives. Love, Kindness, Honour, and Respect give a sacred purpose to life and, in turn, create a life of purpose.

I spent years studying personal development during my university courses, and later within yoga studies. Still, none of that compares to the depths of what my spiritual master taught me through his example and by his affectionate instructions. He gave me access to a more subtle level of personal development and self-realization that equipped me with the skills and tools to learn to honor, love, and respect in trying times of disturbance. Like waves crashing on the surface, life can become turbulent, but through conscious awareness, we can dive deep beneath the crashing waves to the peaceful depths of compassion and tolerance. Let's face it— disruption and disturbances are an inevitable part of life. So, the ability to transcend the turmoil and chaos and access inner peace is an invaluable gift, and the reality is, this incredible ability is available to everyone.

These are the skills and values I hope to share and bring out in all who enter my life. I truly feel life is a precious gift and that the most important thing to bring out in people is the love we have inside us and that we all must learn the value and practical application of being humble and tolerant and giving respect to others. These are the most important values because they bring peace and harmony into our lives.

I have so much gratitude for being taught these lessons at such a young age and am grateful that I could obtain peace even when the circumstances seemed to be so overwhelming. It's best not to take situations personally and to try with all your heart to reflect only love and compassion. My best friend in India, Ranjit Prabhu, is constantly reminding me to be unaffected and harmonized, to send love and affection even to our enemies. This attitude brings me so much peace, *Om Shanti Shanti Om.*

What are these teachings, values, and skills that have transformed my life in such a profound way? Well, it's quite simple, actually: being humbler than a blade of grass, being more tolerant than a tree, and giving respect to others without desiring it for myself.

> ➤ Humility: non-expectation of recognition for our merits and a feeling of being dependent on and blessed by divinity.

> ➤ Tolerance: not allowing ourselves to be disturbed by or to succumb to others' negativity and bearing no ill will towards anyone.

> ➤ Giving respect: recognizing the presence of divinity within all beings and offering respect to others without expecting it to be offered in return.

Practicing these qualities helps you become centered in a humble heart space so you will be satisfied with serving those who inspire you. Serving a personality so dear and precious to the heart brings a lifetime of shelter and guidance. However, to strive to be your best and to give your full authentic self requires the adherence to a prescribed lifestyle that needs to be practiced. In Bhakti yoga, we call this our *Sadhana*, our spiritual practice routine.

My ideal attitude of gratitude daily routine is as follows. I awaken at 4 a.m., which is a very auspicious time of the Bhakti yoga philosophy. This is called the *Brahma Muhurtta* (ninety-six minutes before sunrise) when all of nature is waking with the dawn of the new day. This time of day is within the material mode of goodness. Waking at this naturally peaceful time of the day to engage in our wholesome spiritual practice together as a family fills my heart with such a depth of gratitude for so many reasons.

I feel fortunate to be able to adhere to this ancient wisdom and practice as a family. How rare this is. When raising teenagers, you generally expect that they will offer disrespect and arrogance. You might think they will have an I'm-too-cool-for-school kind of attitude and might want to sleep in until the absolute last minute before they need to go off to school or work. My teens are actually the ones who are enthusiastically waking me up at 4 a.m. for our devotional practice. I start the day at 4 a.m. with a cleansing ritual for my digestive system, and then I go into mantra meditation. Some mornings we walk around our gardens chanting the sacred Hare Krishna mantra quietly and allowing the early morning dew to absorb through the naked soles of our feet. This ritual fills our physical being up with Mother Earth's energy and charges up our immune systems. Interaction with nature, combined with the cleansing sound vibration of mantra meditation, lifts our family to a higher vibration, enabling us to nurture and care for each other so that we can keep up with the high demands of our dynamic and creative lifestyles as artists and business managers. I grew up in a family unit, but now I live within a serving unit of consciousness. As a family, we help each other to resist temptation to acquire, consume, and control—to live a life of dedicated service.

Just before the soothing sunrises, we find personal sacred space to chant the Gayatri Mantra privately. This mantra is given from the spiritual master as a gift and is the ceremony of the second level of initiation. My Gayatri Mantra ceremony was a unique experience that I cherish with my whole heart. My spiritual master, His Divine Grace Govinda Maharaj, was so kind when giving me this mantra. In this ceremony, he directed me on the path to building a global values school based on the principles of Bhakti yoga.

I opened my heart during this initiation. Generally, the student or disciple receiving the second initiation comes with an offering filled with gifts. My unique gift to him, which he very happily accepted, was my whole life as a service offering. How did I express this? I wrote my spiritual teacher a sincere poem. When it comes time for gift-giving, I prefer to make the gift with a personal touch. At this time, the initiation took place in our temple in Nabadwip, West Bengal. There were no art materials available. The only thing I had to write with was my cosmetics and makeup bag. So off I went to write a poem and decorate it with what was at my disposal: colorful eyeliners, eyeshadows, and lipsticks. He had already given me the world and an endless supply of protection and heartfelt exchange. In return, I wanted to offer him something from my heart to show my appreciation and gratitude.

In this sweet and sincere poem, I offered to develop a school to provide education for our mission's next generation. He was so thrilled when I read it to him. It was one of the rarest moments in time I have ever experienced. It was this personalized ceremony that gave me entrance into the path of Bhakti yoga. The shelter and energy the Gayatri Mantra provides are enriched with a type of gentleness and sweetness. In the Vedic philosophy, this is called rasa and ruci, a pure kind of sweetness within the heart's core.

Yes, I am extremely grateful for receiving the sacred Gayatri Mantra, but what actually is gratitude anyway? Gratitude is feedback from the Lord within our hearts, and it's a tangible reality both inside and out. The internal symptom is a love for life. The external symptom is that you receive something, and the appreciation and acknowledgment of that gift is a deep sense of gratitude and thankfulness. True spiritual awareness is a heart-to-heart transaction, and gratitude is literally falling in love with your life.

After our Gayatri mediation, our family meets together in our temple space and we engage with enthusiasm in singing and dancing, which is known as Kirtan. It generally lasts about 40 minutes. Then we offer our breakfast to the altar and engage in our ashtanga yoga, a few yoga sequences to nourish our physical selves. We come back together as a family and sit and take the *mahaprasad (Mercy)*. *Mahaprasad* is a Sanskrit term, meaning "Gracious Gift." It is blessed food that has been offered to God/Goddess and then distributed to the family as a blessing. So I guess you can say our food is filled with love.

Purport: "We cannot bribe the Personality of Godhead. He is so great that our bribery has no value. Nor has He any scarcity; since He is full in Himself, what can we offer Him? He produces everything. We simply offer to show our love and gratitude to the Lord." (SB 3.29.24)

As I sit taking this breakfast prasad with my family, I am sure to be reminded of how fortunate I am to be a mother of four beautiful children who are all inspired to practice Bhakti yoga daily with me. So, for this time of the day, there have been many windows of opportunity to experience glimpses of gratitude and satisfaction.

"God gave you a gift of 86400 seconds today.
Have you used one to say thank you?"

~ William Arthur Ward

If I experience gratitude with a hint of contentment, then if the rest of my day offers a diverse range of circumstances, I can remain unaffected. By valuing self-regulation and commitment to engaging in this morning practice, I can be situated in a very peaceful state of mind. It's as if we are peaceful warriors equipped with weapons of kindness, humility, tolerance, and respect. This early morning sacred practice provides us with access to maintaining the position of being the servants of the servants so that we offer humility, tolerance, and respect to those who come across our paths. The majority of the time, this provides full wellness and a depth of understanding about the self that diffuses any tension or disturbances in the workplace, community, event, or gathering.

"Thankfulness is the beginning of gratitude.
Gratitude is the completion of thankfulness.
Thankfulness may merely consist of words.
Gratitude is shown in acts."

~ Henri Frederic Amiel

As I look back on my life, I can see many episodes of our journey in which we have faced tests and challenges. I see myself being good and kind-hearted and, unfortunately, attracting people who want to exploit me and try to bring me down, especially in the workplace. I question how I could cope with these difficulties and still maintain being a positive, nurturing teacher and personal trainer to my clients. Only by the grace and teaching of my Gurudev could I do so. His example of magnanimity and benevolence has shaped my heart to be forgiving and compassionate. How grateful I am to have a teacher who has provided me the opportunity to have this serving attitude of gratitude.

Earlier I talked about being equipped with weapons to enhance my ability to cope with these tests. This also provides me with endless gratitude to recognize the sweet mercy in seeing that these tests and challenges are simply coming to me because of my own karma. It is a blessing to see that all of the tests are my friends and teachers to discover more truths about myself.

It's a mystical process to go from the level of deep inquiry about the self to the deeper level of investigation—and without any control to be pulled and drawn to a space of the deepest questions and inquiries about one's real self. This has brought me to a state of surrender. This entrance to the deepest places brings the sweet absolute truth. I am not the controller. My real position is to be a sweet servant to the supreme, to serve his devotees with love and affection—a simple process with high thinking. Having my mindset tuned to this way of thinking brings about a mystical transformation that continually unfolds daily. A realm of bliss and eternal gratitude can be accessed. However, it's up to me to turn on the receptors and receive this love, mercy, and guidance.

So, I pray now that you, too, as you are reading, are questioning two things. Where and what is this blissful realm she is talking about? How can someone be given a consistent share of trials and tribulations but still maintain a space of being unaffected?

In the Vedas, this place of bliss is called *Satcitananda.* That is *Sat* (truth), *Cit* (eternity), and *Ananda* (high).

This is a place in time and space that is accessible to anyone. But how does one get there, and what road would you take? I encourage all seekers of the truth to ask these questions and check in with these questions daily.

My way of finding bliss is so simple and sweet. By valuing gratitude and service to the supreme personality and his devotees, I know this is my way to gaining access to this place of bliss. Each of us has our own sacred place where we meditate or take ourselves for spiritual rest. The place I take myself within my heart and mind is Sri Nabadwip Dham, my spiritual master's ashram in West Bengal, India. The bliss there is indescribable, and the devotees there are the sweetest, kindest, and most caring people I have ever met.

Have you heard of love in separation? I used to go through an extreme separation when I would return home from a retreat in Bali or from visiting the ashram in India. But after many long heartfelt conversations with my best friend in India, Ranjit Prabhu, he taught me to be grateful for the realization that Sri Nabadwip Dham is accessible wherever I may be. He has taught me to see this place as a state of consciousness and apply it to every minute of my day, that I can close my eyes and enter Nabadwip if I am in the right serving mood. This ashram is seriously my heaven on earth. I always planned to live at Sri Nabadwip by the banks of the Ganges. You have to believe if you are to manifest these transcendental ideas. I am now dedicating my time and working hard to develop an eco-village and holistic school in this blissful Nabadwip community in India.

After 15 years of making this offering to my beloved spiritual master, my heart's desire is finally manifesting. By seeking out sincere, quality guidance and support, I have now developed such a dynamic project that will display my mood of gratitude. I am helping to create inspiring and loving spaces for the next generation to thrive in, and it is finally all falling into place, by the will of his sweet grace. This eco-village will have an online college, sustainable agroforestry farm, eco-retreat, wellness hub, and a production company where young people will be hosting music and dance events.

Through all my personal struggles this current year during the COVID pandemic, I have had the privilege of watching our community's next generation create some blissful soul-searching tunes. My son, Keziah Sundar, is a production company manager and produces good-vibe tracks under the performing name 3FORM. This year's tracks have been my salvation. This year, I took a work contract overseas and was isolated during that time and had to quarantine for two weeks. Keziah's creative tunes were my catalyst in getting back to that blissful state of consciousness.

For the past seven years, he and I together have hosted music and dance festivals for young people on their soul-searching journeys. The pandemic has restricted us from being able to host a festival or event all year. This is another example of love in separation. I really miss these fun and dynamic events. I am so grateful for the number of events we were able to host. I had the privilege of being the Community Mumma looking out for these beautiful young adults who desire to be in an environment that provides them with a unique sense of belonging.

My son designs these events as his unique way of channeling our spiritual masters' love. I am so grateful that he has adapted to the pandemic's current changes, developing an audience and expanding his followers online. He is a scarce soul, and I am so blessed to call him my son and my god brother and my business partner.

I have people ask me why I support these youth events, and I simply reply, "I view this as a necessary service." My spiritual master encourages this type of service, reminding me that "the children are our fortune and are our future." As challenging as these festivals and events can be, I maintain a sense of purpose when I share this amazing experience with my son. I have a substantial appreciation for dance and music, and these festivals and events are a way for me to share that gratitude.

**"Then that supreme authority, personified by
sound and unseen by eyes,
but most wonderful, stopped speaking. Feeling
a sense of gratitude,
I offered my obeisances unto Him, bowing my
head."**

(SB 1.6.25)

Gratitude has the potential to offer so much grace and peace to
one's vision. I have often heard my spiritual master remind us of
the importance of adjusting our angle of vision to not quarrel with
the environment. On many occasions, I have been extremely
fortunate to be reminded of this life lesson to adapt my own vision
during conflicting times at gatherings and community events. To
walk away from the conflict unaffected makes one feel victorious,
while at the same time so harmonized with the environment and
the overflowing nectar of gratitude. I feel that I shine most at the
Nabadwip Ashram and at my son's festivals and in those places
where my true serving nature is appreciated in return.

**"Gratitude is a powerful catalyst for happiness.
It's the spark that lights joy in your soul."**

~ Amy Collette

"When we focus on our gratitude, the tide of disappointment goes out, and the tide of love rushes in."

~ Kristin Armstrong

CHAPTER SEVEN

Gratitude Multitude
An Attitude of Gratitude
Wake up Call

By Patrick Oei

Feelings, in hindsight, give us the best in everything as we reflect upon the happenings that come our way. Though painful, though laughable, though inspirational, it boils down to being grateful for the many blessings that come our way. It may sound painful along the way, but when it is over, one can never be grateful enough for the bountiful blessings that come along the way.

Come for Coffee

A message from the receptionist: *Pls call the doctor at this number.*

I calmly walked to the company's factory's warehouse office, of which I'm the Chief Operating Officer.

"Good Morning, Doctor?" I greeted him. After all the pleasantries, he asked me to go to his office for coffee and chit-chat. I told him, "Please tell me my wife's diagnosis." He said, "No, you come to my office for coffee." I told him, "It's okay, you may tell me." This went on a few times.

In the end, I asked him, "Does my wife have leukemia?" There was dead silence on the other end for quite a few seconds. Instead of shocking me, he was shocked and lost for words that I knew the answer. I told him "It's okay. You may tell me, Doc."

After a while, he spoke up, "How did you know the diagnosis?"

"I used to visit my fellow parishioners and pray for them with my group. Based on the bone marrow and lumbar puncture tests you conducted, it's very obvious. One with leukemia does these two tests quite often, and I have become familiar with them."

In the end, he replied, "That is correct." My world crashed. I had to sit down as I was standing speaking to him. My eyes welled up with tears and my voice cracked.

I asked what the options were, moving forward. One of the options was to transfer her to a government hospital for long term care, as the costs would be phenomenal, even in a government hospital, but especially a private hospital.

It was a whirlwind series of tests and tests. Chemotherapy followed with all the known side-effects thereafter. My wife says she could take the pain, but like all cancer patients, the loss of **her hair** was a crushing blow. This diagnosis came four months after the birth of our son. She knew hair loss would be one of the effects of any chemotherapy and yet, when it happened, it was indeed devastating emotionally.

I decided to print my baby's photos and pin them on the wall right in front of the bed. It was meant to fortify her resolve to fight it. This served as the rallying call of the fight against cancer, which would last for ten long, long years. It was indeed painful and a whirlwind sad experience for anyone.

It was indeed a challenge. In hindsight, I'm grateful that my perspective of life changed so much after that. It was no longer about money and wealth, but about her and my son. The first three years and the last two years were the most painful, excruciating experiences, which I don't wish upon anyone else. It became a daily routine of being in the hospital in the morning, and then work, and then hospital again. I was doing my MBA at that time and it was also study time at the hospitals. On top of that, I was doing part-time lecturing at a few institutions of higher learning. It's a wonder that I got my master's with High Honors. After a year, I stopped lecturing.

Initially, I was like a zombie—work, hospital, home to be with the baby boy. I guess it was the most challenging period of my life.

How does one grapple with this routine for three years? After three years, she went into remission, which provided a breather for me.

Blessing in Disguise

The best twist in this episode was having my mum and my sisters come over to stay with us to help look after the boy, with a domestic helper in tow.

This twist of events was good as it helped my boy learn yet another language the Malay language, though patois in some ways. And that made him multi-lingual later on.

I went to take Japanese classes with him. He didn't follow up on this as he was too busy with his schoolwork. I'm sure he will be able to pick it up in the future when the need arises, but learning German at a higher secondary level was good for him. This was in addition to learning English as a first language and Mandarin (Chinese) as a second language.

I taught him many skills, like numeracy skills in a playful manner while rolling on the floor. I also taught him excellent typing skills; when he entered Secondary 1, he was so dexterous with his typing that he was able to type with ten fingers compared to his peers. Whether he knows it or not, I embarked on a mission to equip him with skills that he could use to be independent and harness his potential and abilities in many forms.

I remember struggling with Enid Blyton's books in Primary 6, but he could read it in Primary 1 almost effortlessly. Being lazy yet smart, he would gloss over many words, guessing their meaning along the way and occasionally looking some up in the dictionary. I knew he skipped looking them up, but, after a while, he became so good at just understanding meaning by guessing.

In Primary 2, I decided to buy him a *Hardy Boys* book, knowing it was going to be so tricky because I was struggling with many of those words in Secondary 2. He looked at the book and tried reading it and said it was too difficult for him and threw it aside.

Two months later, he decided to look it up and read it … and came up to me to ask if I could buy him more *Hardy Boys* books. That request was the best news to me. I gleefully went to buy more of such books from this series for him. This is a blessing as it augmented his mastery of the English language. That put him in a good position to write articles for the Mainstream Straits Times for the YouthInk series, which got students to pen articles for other students. This paid a bit and was a good introduction into copywriting for him, I suppose. I am glad he is quite a prolific writer and reader today.

This brings me to his formative years in kindergarten and lower primary school. I would incorporate study into playtimes to assimilate new learning, like memorizing the Times Table, i.e., the Multiplication Tables, spelling new words, and long words.

Upbringing is also a challenge as sometimes we are faced with what is right and what may not go well with the issue of values. I remember attending a Les Misérables concert with him and his late mum when he was seven years old. After the show, while walking to the car park, we realized that some of the merchandise that we had bought was not charged to our credit card. My wife and I discussed whether to go back to inform them of the short-charge and the implication on the staff and possible reprimand from his bosses. Our son interjected with "Isn't it right to return?" We knew then that this boy would grow up with the right values. The attitude of gratitude overwhelmed us that day.

Being both a mother and a father after his mum's death at the same time is not easy, after his mum's death. It means I have to be the authoritative figure, yet the loving part has to surface to balance his upbringing. I remember instilling in him this notion that it is okay for a boy and, for the matter, an adult, to kiss his dad at home and even in public. And I'm glad he does so without inhibitions. After training him to take public transportation to school in his secondary school days, I only drove him to school during exam days to give him extra sleep time.

One could see the stares from the other parents' car, stares of amazement and envy, when he kissed me before alighting from my car. You can bet many of them wish this upon themselves, to be able to have their kids kiss them in public. I remember telling him if anyone teases you about this, it's because their parents don't do it to them. Surprisingly, none of his classmates teased him about it.

One particular incident really amazed me and still stuns me to this day. I was one of the speakers at the Hwa Chong Junior College seminar for parents and kids. During the buffer reception after the sharing, while I was speaking with his favorite teacher, he came up to me and said he was leaving with his friends to go to a nearby games arcade. And, without any inhibition, he came up to me to kiss me on my cheek. And of course, I returned one kiss. It was the best day of my life for a long time to have him do that. Though, I must say that this has lessened so much into his adulthood.

An attitude of gratitude taught me that if we imbue the right values and correct upbringing, we will get the right results.

Seeing him enter a governmental gifted program was the best gift to me. He could not utter a single word in Mandarin when he entered Kindergarten as both of us weren't conversant in it. The Chinese language has become important in Singapore and globally. I was super glad that he placed in well to master the Chinese Language, i.e., Mandarin. He continued with this gifted program right up until GCE "O" levels. While most students take the Chinese O levels exam in Secondary 4, he took it at Secondary 3, received distinctions, and proceeded to take Higher Chinese GCE

"O" levels in Secondary 4. In the end, he took 12 O levels during Secondary 4. What an intelligent kid.

His scholarship award by the Public Service Commission of the Government of Singapore was the best news a parent could receive. However, he was almost offered other scholarships, including from the SPH, the leading and largest mainstream newspaper publisher in Singapore.

I am happy that though he was asked to go to the final interview, he wanted to inform them that he would be withdrawing from this interview as he instead chose to accept the PSC scholarship. Even when I tested him that they will have someone on the reserve list to award to if he declines after being accepted, he said he didn't want to waste their time and deprive others of a first choice offer. Likewise, he withdrew from the Jurong Town Corporation Scholarship.

We Need to Help Ourselves to Help Others

In order to help others, one needs to also help oneself. This is where I was glad to happen upon an organization that helped inspire me in more ways than one.

Joining Toastmasters helped me gain some sanity as it gave me a boost every 1st and 3rd Wednesday of the month, and it helped inspire me each time to hear many great speeches, many of which were practical, motivating, and inspirational. Indeed, it was a tough experience after the initial few years of going to work, hospital, home, work, and hospital.

That's where I met someone who told me that caregivers need some space and time for themselves as they may get resentful after a while. No, I was not bitter, but I was hurt that God would allow this to happen to me and my family, to suffer like this.

Yet, I am so grateful for the many friends and benefactors who were sources of strength and inspiration to my family and me.

There are indeed many days and nights when I fall into deep depression and loneliness before and after her death. I had to live for her and my son, to do my best for him.

My confidence is shaken up by such frustration as I wallow in it. But, like a light at the end of the tunnel, after she passed on, I knew that she'd be a blessing to my son and me.

Oh my, Mama

One dreadful morning, at about 3 am, I saw my mum on the floor and moved. Calling and awaiting the ambulance's arrival was tragic and painful. It took about 45 minutes for the ambulance to arrive. Despite all the electric pumping, they could not revive her after 15 minutes. I told them off, told them to let her go in peace. They were too late, and my marvelous mum, whom I still miss until today, had passed on.

I had to wait until morning to go to the nearby clinic to get a doctor to certify her death, go to the newspaper office to book an obituary ad, make arrangements with the funeral company for the wake and funeral, and then go to the hospital to visit my wife, whom my mum loved dearly, just like her own daughter.

Her first words to me were, "Why are you wearing all black?" and my reply was, "Mum passed away this morning." I had just come from the press office after booking the obituary ad. We both had a good cry that morning. Five hours later, I was back home to receive her corpse after embalming in a nice coffin I chose for her earlier.

It was painful as my wife wanted to pay her last respects to Mum, but the doctors disallowed it as she was not well, and her immunity was too low to visit her. She was an awesome daughter-in-law to my mum, and my mum really loved and treasured her a lot. I visited her each morning and consoled her, telling her not to worry and that I was sure Mum visited her in the hospital during those days too and was blessing her lots.

The first three years and the last two years were the most challenging and most overwhelmingly absorbing. The last year was when she deteriorated into a vegetable. She was bedridden and was unable to even sit up on her own. That's when I applied to have a second domestic maid to help prop her up to feed her. The approval was not forthcoming, and I had to appeal several times for the approval. In the end, I had to seek one of my neighbors to come over at lunchtime each day to aid the present helper and to prop her up to feed her when I was not able to be at home.

It was so sad and depressing to see her in such a state. But, the marriage vows "For better or for worse" really comes into mind and play. It is easy to utter such words, and I can assure you that in those trying moments, even just recalling them, the pain and the trauma of seeing her suffer, will bring tears back. Writing this story is a personal challenge to help me pour out the hidden feelings bottled up all these years. And I am indeed grateful to be able to pen this as a form of therapy, too.

One has overcome these pains, but one is never sure when one has overcome these painful moments and the grief of losing someone one loves and adores.

This brings back memories of our first few memories of how we met in the church of a youth group I founded. I had taken up the challenge of organizing a Christmas treat for children and she was my vice-chairman. We faced the opportunities to work together, the meetings thereafter, which became dates after that, and the challenges of a relationship in which I was the younger man and her family objected to our relationship.

For those of you reading this, I would like you to join me in penning the names of 100 to 200 of your friends and family whom you want to express your gratitude to for helping you grow during those periods and now as you mature.

Gratitude to my True Friends

I am indebted to the people who helped me then and now. Sometimes, the encouraging words, the comforting touch, and deeds one extends to you are so overwhelmingly helpful. To those of you, I say a big thanks, merci, terima kasih, xie xie, nandrii.

Yes, you will never know how much you have made me a better person.

It is in moments when you are down and out that you realize who your true friends are. I am grateful to the friends who supported, encouraged, and inspired me, through thick and thin, during those times when hope seemed hopeless and tears seemed endless.

There was also an episode in which an old lady doesn't know and understand what leukemia is. She went to share with a common friend to avoid as she thinks that such survivors are infectious. This friend told her off, saying that her concerns are indeed misplaced. Hearing of this, I can only say, "Forgive her Lord for she knows not what she is saying."

Just as I'm wrapping up this story, it goes around one full circle. I had a small pimple that seemed harmless. And it grew and became painful. After a week, I went to the doctor and was prescribed antibiotics. It didn't abate after another week. Then I went to the Polyclinic for more treatment. Guess what happened? I was told to go to the accidents and emergency unit of the Singapore General Hospital and was told I needed an operation to remove it.

And I couldn't believe it. I was placed in the same ward that my 1st late wife was during those ten years, 98% of the time. It was an emotional roller coaster as I grappled with it.

It goes full circle.

It makes me wonder, why here? Why now as I'm finishing up this chapter for this book.

I'm not sure if my son has the same feelings as he probably remembers the visits, especially during the last four or five years, as he was growing up to see his late mum.

It took me a while to ponder, reflect, and pray over this. This may be meant to empower me with the extra strength to plod on for my next phase of life. Having encountered so much, I always tell those around me that I don't want to live beyond 60, although I'm reaching 61 soon. Maybe God has a higher purpose for me. One can't imagine the sad memories as I type these few paragraphs, as tears well up within me. *Why this same block when she passed away in this block...* I can't recall if it's really the same ward—it was 24 years ago from this 2020 COVID period.

It gives me the courage to ponder even more that we just have to appreciate our loved ones, near and far, and treasure them more. Life is unpredictable.

Moral of the Story

On a parting note, let me share this story of a musician who lived in a resort island and composed his own songs, as well as performed pop songs at a hotel lounge for a minimum wage.

A tourist asks him how often he performs. "Three times a week," he answered.

He made enough for himself and his family.

Tourist asked" him, "What do you do at other times?"

"I sleep late, spend time with the children, with my partner. Meet friends for coffee. Enjoy the sea and time with nature."

The tourist said, "I have an MBA from Harvard; let me share how you can make money."

"You should perform more shows each week. With the extra revenue, you can buy better equipment to sell your music online, and with more money, you can employ a manager, a promoter, and a personal assistant. Instead of local shows, you can sell your music overseas. You can go to New York, Los Angeles, Vegas, London. From there, you can do anything you desire."

"How long would that take?" asked the Musician. "Twenty to twenty-five years," the tourist answered.

The musician then asked him, "And after that?"

Well, my friend, that's when it gets interesting. You can buy and sell stocks and property and make millions more.

Again, the musician asked, "And after that?"

The tourist answered, "After that, you can retire, you can sleep late, spend time with the children, with your partner in a resort. Meet friends for coffee. Enjoy the sea and time with nature."

The musician answered, "With all due respect, sir, that's exactly what we are doing now. Why do I want to waste 25 years to arrive at this? I already have it."

The moral of the story is sometimes less is more and sometimes more is less.

Each time we board an airplane, the boarding safety instructions tell us to put on an oxygen mask first before doing it for our children or aged parents. Why is that so? Because only when you are alive can you help them. Imagine if you put on the oxygen mask for your kid and then you pass out or conk out—will they be able to put it on for you? Will you make them panic even more? In their haste, they may also remove their masks, not knowing they need it.

The moral of the story is that we need to look after ourselves and love ourselves more to look after our loved ones.

I would like to share with you these takeaways:

Love yourself.

Appreciate your loved ones, your benefactors.

Savor each moment. Spend time with them.

Be in touch and contact with them.

Reach out to them regularly, so that you don't regret not doing things with them after they are gone.

Express your love for them.

Express your appreciation for your loved ones and especially to your friends and benefactors.

"Remember that what you now have was once among the things you only hoped for."

~ Epicurus

CHAPTER EIGHT

Discovering Gratitude

By Jacinta Legg

Have you noticed and not forgotten that time when someone has just gone out of their way to do something kind for you? How did that make you feel? Or when you, in fact, did something that made someone else feel appreciative and thankful? Those warm and fuzzy feelings inside? What are they?

That's the feeling of gratitude. We can feel gratitude in parts of our lives naturally towards people or things, but we can also experience these warm fuzzy feelings more throughout our lives. It doesn't have to be a memory or something you don't see or do much of. It can be something you include in your life to help cultivate a better way of living, meaning a better quality of life, to help you feel happier and more fulfilled within your life and not just in segments.

Are you sick of hardships knocking you back a few steps or interfering with your positive emotions? Do you want to step outside your comfort zone and adventure into the unknown? Or maybe you just want to feel better and think better? I think we all can be our higher selves and create the lives we want to live. So what is it going to take? If I were to say there is a way of making this and doing this, would you follow?

If I were to say there is a secret door to greater happiness and health, would you want the key?

Would you be thankful for the key? Before you knew what was on the other side?

If you said yes, then you're the first step of the way. If you said no, is it due to me needing to convince you more? Or because you're distrustful of what could happen next or of what I am saying? Think about this! It doesn't matter what someone tells you or does for you; it's how they're doing it or how you're going to react to that situation, which could, in turn, change the outcome. Of course, if someone gave me a secret key and waited for me to open the door to see if I was thankful or not, that would not exactly be an act of gratitude for me. Still, if the person wanted to help me as an act of kindness, and therefore, I was open to receiving that, there would be no hesitation upfront, and I would go forth to grab that key to unlock that door.

People are more willing to listen and act when gratitude reflects from within you. When you are grateful, you will see more appreciation. You can use it in business, throughout your personal life, or even for how you think about the world itself.

Gratitude allows you to feel more positive emotions and truly relish the good experiences over the not-so-good, enabling you to be more grateful for your life and the people within it. This allows us to unlock a greater energy for ourselves.

Being grateful for who you are, where you are, and what you are in life are the key ingredients to living a more abundant life. Being thankful for what we have had in our lives is truly the next step to finding your inner peace. We can all do this even if we are not feeling so great. However, it will start to make you feel more generous and happier than you were before you started this process.

An attitude of gratitude will determine your level of altitude in your life. Think about that.

If you think you cannot or do not want to try this, then simply try to reverse this thinking process and see what happens. Why not just tell yourself that you are going to be open to it rather than not? Reverse the psychology of your own brain. If it's going to bring more gratitude to you and that means more happiness and a better way of life, then surely you're going to give it a go! It depends on your own reasons for finding your gratitude. If you don't know what they are, then listen to yourself and those signals inside of you. What do you truly desire?

Why not try to be kinder on a day-to-day basis, regardless? Kindness is the first natural step to cultivating gratitude and making the process more natural and relaxed to follow.

This will start to change the way you focus on the positive rather than the negative. You'll also notice the difference in how you feel and in everyone else around you.

It actually takes less energy to be kind and thankful than to be unkind and unthankful. What I have learned is that the more we appreciate, the less we expect, dictate, and focus our attention on the "I cannot" instead of the "I can." We can then redirect that focus on what we can achieve, what we can build, what it is that we truly desire. All these positive reinforcements play a big part in gratitude and finding your own.

The Secret to the Attitude of Gratitude

I think most of us would know that the more you practice something, the better you get, the more natural it becomes. Practice makes perfect, right! To become happier and more fulfilled, there is an attitude of gratitude that can easily be adapted into your everyday life. Anybody can adopt this process. It just takes consistency and the willingness to want to be happier with what you have.

The secret is a process that you must commit to, follow, and adapt into your daily life. We can do this with any of the following points below. For example:

- Wake up every morning and say thank you for being alive. Start doing this every day.

- Start a gratitude journal. Write a list of all the things you are grateful for on a daily-to-weekly basis.

- Create a grateful home environment, love where you live.

- Appreciate everything and try not to be so picky.

- Be more giving and give back to people who were there for you.

- Practice mindfulness and gratefulness for at least eight weeks. This can help you rewire your brain naturally to lead to more happiness.

- Find gratitude in your challenges (the harder it is upfront, the easier it will become).

- Volunteer or help the less fortunate than you.

- Express yourself to others. Don't just keep your gratitude inside. Let it flow.

- beautifully from within.

- Spend time with loved ones regularly.

- Improve your happiness in other areas of your life—not just what is already.

- making you happy. Refocus it as we can always turn a weakness into a strength.

- Complain less and find the solution to the problem.

- Don't overthink everything.

- Watch your words when you speak to others. Don't assume all the time; ask the question.

- Have less screen time and more real time with family and friends.

- Create a vision board in your home or your office of daily tasks and events you are grateful for.

- Set some goals; start achieving. Without goal setting, how are we to know what we truly want to achieve?

You can also use gratitude in other areas of your life where it may not be so present.

The past. Retrieve positive memories and be thankful for your life rather than unthankful; tap into your inner self (child) and learn from the experiences that have caused you pain. Accept them and let them help you face your fears. (There are courses on EFT matrix reimprinting techniques that teach you how to do this if needed.)

The future. Maintain a hopeful and optimistic attitude, regardless of someone's inherent or current level of gratitude. Practice your affirmations, set your goals, complete your to-do lists, count your wins, write thank you notes, meditate, eat well, exercise. All this will help in making you feel more focused and grateful. There may be instances when you're not always going to keep up with all these tasks all at the same time, but making an effort to include them can be key to transforming your life to what you want it to be. All these things will help you feel better at achieving more appreciation in your life and, even better, more gratitude. Don't let people embitter you, and don't let hardships scar you. Remember, learn from these experiences and feel good for yourself and others around you, too.

The Key

The key to making this happen and unlocking that door is to **commit** yourself and to practice these points daily. **Begin** finding your own and writing them down. What are you grateful for? You don't need to know all of this at once, so start adding them daily or weekly, depending on your schedule. It will begin to build up and you will start to see all the parts of your life you are grateful for. **Feel it** some days. You may not feel great, depending on your attitude. That's okay, just do it anyway, and, when you can, sit there and reflect on how much better that made you feel. Move into the feeling, dance it, sing it, and tell yourself why you are doing it. **Please write it down** as a reminder when you're feeling less energized. Writing is a fun way to remind yourself rather than looking at a screen. Set yourself gratitude reminders if need be. Find a fun way to adapt these techniques so that you'll actually want to do them.

When you think about starting a new process or doing something different, it can quite easily be off-putting, but remember, change for the better is good. The more you do something, the more natural it becomes. When you think of autopilot, what comes to your mind?

Remember how scary it was when you first drove a car, or how much focus was needed? Then gradually, you started to become more confident. It then becomes easier. This is a similar process. Your autopilot is your natural reaction and way of doing things.

Having gratitude within your autopilot is key, so adapt this into your schedule. Make more time for it to become a natural process.

Shaping Your Whole

Who is in control of your life, words, actions, beliefs, and mindset?

You are. So own it! Take control and enjoy it. The power we all have inside us needs exercising and guidance, discipline, routine, balance, love, and care. It's what we have inside us that is us, which becomes who we are.

Belief systems play a significant role in who we are. If we select our beliefs based on positive and effective ones, it will help our lives become fuller and humbler. One of my beliefs, for example, is "I believe in my life and being happy" and sharing that with the ones I love and care about. This is a belief I firmly live by: I treat people how I wish to be treated. That is one I was raised with from a very young age and has always been quite useful for me. Recreate this based on what you want in life.

Focus on the positive over the negative—it's the only way to believe.

Take control, turn your life into a positive one, do what you enjoy more often, and do what makes you happy. I've found a strategy to help me keep up with all this. These methods have positively impacted me. I have used most of these points to achieve a happier state of wellbeing.

I had a hard year last year when my mother got diagnosed with stage three lung cancer. I found that life became quite frail and upsetting very quickly. My usual self and energy levels were down, and my happiness was spiked by an unhappy feeling that I had felt for quite some time from finding out about my mother's cancer.

My relationship was also testing me, and I was responsible for being a mother to two beautiful children under the age of three. I needed to keep my happiness and wellbeing up for them, even though I was not feeling up to it. I started setting goals and planning out what I would do to help fix what I could. I decided to go back to work and challenge myself and become more financially stable. I decided to make every day better and better until it became better. I decided I did not want to feel so down anymore and replaced those feeling with good feelings. I pledged to myself to reverse the situation for my health and wellbeing for my children and me. My mother's treatment then became more promising, my work life became easier, and I adapted more over time. I started hitting my targets, achieving what I set out for myself, and now I'm feeling great, even though I'm based in Melbourne and we're all feeling the backlash from lockdown. For me, life has been great, but for some, I can imagine it is not so great. So why not try using gratitude as a way of feeling better through these hard times or use gratitude to unlock your inner chi.

I have managed to use these strategies in this chapter to enhance my life and wellbeing to get where I am now, feeling happy and optimistic, even though my mother still has cancer. I am currently living in a lockdown in Melbourne, Australia. I have listed some other methods you can use to improve your own gratitude.

A Focus

A focus has always been the number one savior for me, to get me up and not down. This can really help focus your attention on the positive rather than the negative if you don't know what you want to do. Really dive deep into this to find your focus, your drive, interests, and goals.

What makes you happy? How are you going to get there? How can you get yourself there? To satisfy our gratitude, we need to make time for ourselves too.

Focus on the things that make you feel good! The things that positively distract you and make you feel good from the inside out! You know what they are. So, think, take action, and move forward with a positive distraction!

A Healthy Diet

Eating food that makes you feel good is so essential for nourishing yourself and feeling fulfilled. What we put into our body is priceless, as we're investing in our health and longevity... Of course, we would all like to be able to afford organic produce and drink sparkling mineral water every day, but at the same time, don't let that be the reason why you don't! It really goes without saying. It's about transforming a lousy diet into a healthy diet and feeling the success that only you will feel.

This may be on the 'I'll do it later' list but don't forget about setting those goals and working towards it now as it will make you feel more grateful for your body straight away! Take a step into gratitude within your diet and eat a veggie salad or juice daily, for example; you will feel better. It may also start to improve those bad eating habits too. The more you feel good, the more you want to eliminate the not so feeling good.

In 2020, good food tastes better anyway.

Exercise and Fitness

Finding a way to work up a sweat physically can have significant positive effects. We all know it's easier said than done. It's the effort you need to put in that pays off. When you put the time and energy into being grateful for your physical body, you don't have time to tear it apart. When you feel down on yourself, you can choose to indulge in that self-depreciation, or you can employ gratitude to help you shift your mindset. As you start to care for your body through exercise, you will feel more grateful for the body you're living in.

Balance

Many elements in your life contribute to your overall balance. We need it in everything; this is something I have found myself in my personal life, through work life, and even with diet, health, fitness, and relationships. Finding the balance in everything is important in feeling less stressed, more satisfied, and humbler. Balance gives you the tools to help you not feel the need to binge or make drastic decisions based on an emotional response. It's essential to identify the aspects of your life that are imbalanced and deal with them. Find a sensible way to involve things you enjoy while still living a healthy and happy lifestyle. It might be in the food you eat or how much you exercise. Whether it's a little or a lot, there's a balance in everything; understanding this can open doors for you to build your resilience and happiness.

Too much of anything isn't right, and not enough of something is just as bad; the middle ground is just right! Remember that!

Routine, Structure, and Discipline

Establishing a routine helps you work these techniques into your daily life. Make your focus, health, personal balance, and happiness part of your regular pattern, and it will be easier to keep them up over time. This kind of discipline is only going to take you further in life. Having this and being focused is the key to unlocking success.

Laughter and Happiness

Laugh often.

Surround yourself with people who enjoy your company and vice versa. Focusing your attention on things that make you feel good is vital! Add this into your spare time—in the morning, evening, or at the end of your day. We can all do this. It does not cost a thing, but the difference it can have on the way we feel is priceless. When you laugh, you release endorphins that stimulate your serotonin, which encourages a better mood and feel-good factor for yourself and others. Who doesn't want to feel happy? Trust me! If you want something enough, you will make it happen. Determination and manifestation will get you there, and the rest will be history. Listen to the things that make you feel happy, and learn from the things that don't.

Creating your gratitude attitude should be fun, so enjoy the journey, experiment, and find ways that make it more enjoyable for you.

I found this great poem, which expresses what gratitude can do for people's lives.

"Gratitude unlocks the fullness of life. It turns what we have into enough...and more.

It can turn a meal into a feast, a house into a home, a stranger into a friend.

Gratitude makes sense of our past, brings peace for today and creates a vision for tomorrow."

~ Melody Beattie

Just remember: Knowledge is power, the power is within you, kindness is the greatness, and greatness is gratitude.

"If the only prayer you said in your whole life was, 'thank you', that would suffice."

~ Meister Eckhart

CHAPTER NINE

Cancer and Gratitude

By Tina Louise Vercillo

I t just so happens to be spring, my favorite season of the year here in Australia. I'm sitting on a deck chair in my little backyard, sipping Rosehip tea from my special mug, imprinted with the eloquent words `Do what you Love' and trimmed in gold, that my dearest friend Sharon Pearson gave me. The cherry blossoms are opening. The evergreens are luscious. A Japanese inspired bamboo fence and sculptures are dotting the garden bed. A beautiful azure sky scattered with white fluffy clouds float above me. I draw in a long deep breath and take in the beauty of nature that surrounds me. In this moment I have everything I need in life; I feel eternally grateful and completely content... oh no...wait, there it is, the final piece... my daughter's laughter playing subtly in my ears like the most uplifting music coming from inside our home. Now I feel complete. I exhale, and my heart is joyfully beaming with gratitude...

Now, let me take you back to that dreaded day; my "bestest friend" in "da whole wide world" was there sitting right beside me. Think back to all those teenage movies where two best friends are inseparable, doing absolutely everything together, sharing unconditional love, two peas in a pod, and unquestionably soul mates. Well, that's exactly what I have in Nevine. She is sitting by my side in the specialist's room, as she always has, through every high and every low that life has been thrown my way, and today was no different. I can't express in words how lucky I am to have Nevine in my life; she continues to be vital in my journey to wellness. The specialist was sitting on the other side of his desk, wearing a standard grey suit and my file was opened in front of him. His usual calm demeanor was not there today; he looked uncomfortable. It was evident that he just wanted to get to the reason I was at this appointment, and to be frank, so did I. The following words that came out of his mouth stopped me in my tracks: "It's malignant." I had gone in to have a biopsy the week before after having found a lump in my left breast. My specialist knew my family history, so I'm sure that was what made him so uncomfortable in having to tell me that I was the third sister to have breast cancer.

Like, what are the fucking odds... three of three! Seriously?!?

Instantly, tears welled in my eyes, and Nevine and I both sat there looking at each other in complete and utter shock, crying. She reached over and grabbed my hand, squeezed it tightly, looked at me without saying a single word, her eyes piercing my soul, shouting, *You're going to be okay babe.* And like never before, my heart was filled with gratitude that she was there with me.

When life throws you a curve ball, you need to muster with all your might, to find gratitude in an experience like this, even if you are someone that would normally be very positive and easily find the silver lining in daily mundane experiences, just as I did. This time though, I had to dig so deep, I had to navigate through the stream of questions that were getting tangled in my mind.

What did I do wrong?
How can this be happening to me, too?
How do I tell my nine-year-old daughter?
How do I tell my parents this news for a third time?
What treatment plan should I follow?
Am I REALLY going to be okay?

It felt like I was being swept up in a tornado, filled with every single emotion that has ever been attached to fear. It was making me feel nauseous and dizzy.

STOP! I heard my inner voice scream.

You. Did. Nothing. Wrong. You will get through this; take one step at a time. Remember those profound words that Sharon taught us at the Life Coaching intake weekend: "Say yes, and work out the how later. Firstly, just say YES, and we will work out the how later, promise!"

Life won't always go to plan; trust in the process. Experiences won't always make sense in the moment. Trust in the process anyway. Be okay knowing that there may never be a logical answer or explanation to help guide you, and then, trust in the process anyway.

You may have heard Rhonda Byrne say, "There is always something to be grateful for." Where do you sit with that; do you agree with it? Is there always something to be grateful for? Before we can genuinely consider the answer, we should first understand the word's true meaning.

The Oxford online dictionary states:

> gratitude
> /ˈgratɪtjuːd/
> "The quality of being thankful; readiness to show appreciation for and to return kindness."

I would like to add another variation to the meaning as I have learned to understand it myself over the years. I have found that gratitude can also come from an experience, without having the presence or action taking place by another human being. For me, gratitude also comes from the simplest of things, being in awe of perfection in nature, without having to do something kind in return.

So, let's go back now and answer the question: Is there always something to be grateful for? Perhaps the response is more complex, because initially I would have simply replied, "No! There isn't always something to be grateful for." In my mind I thought, *Who would find gratitude in suffering or in losing a loved one?* Upon reflection, and having experienced what I have, especially over more recent years, I can honestly now say that yes, there is absolutely always SOMETHING to be grateful for!

Now... If you allow, I would like to take you on parts of my journey that helped me arrive at that way of thinking.

Gratitude was something that I had to learn. In my opinion, it's a practiced trait. I wasn't born with the ability to just be grateful, however, the more I practiced it, the better I became at it. Just like anything, really, you start as an apprentice and keep practicing your craft until you become the master at it. I'm certainly no master, so I will continue to practice the attitude of gratitude daily, with the hope that one day I may even just master it.

Going back to Rhonda Byrne's saying, sometimes it can be mighty challenging to find gratitude in an experience that just seems unfair, unwanted, and downright gut-wrenching.

Seriously, who would find a single glimmer of gratitude in being told that they have breast cancer at the young age of 40? With their best life still ahead of them! Who would find gratitude in that?

Well... ME... that's who.

Let's be clear here: The gratitude around my cancer journey didn't happen right away. It took time to process everything, to create a space where I could open my heart and mind, and to see the possibilities and opportunities that would in time be presented to me. They would begin to appear as beautifully colored pieces of a jigsaw puzzle, each piece appearing and finding its place in my life through divine timing, to reveal an image of a new body, a new mind, and a soul transforming right before my very eyes. It was nothing short of magical, and the best part of it all—I was the one creating it.

It's an interesting experience telling someone for the first time that I have cancer. I must allow them to have their 'first reaction.' After all, I have had the time to process all of my emotions up to that point, and they are hearing about it for the first time. I use the word "interesting," because, when I shared the news with family and friends, I received responses across the full spectrum of possible reactions. Some would immediately break into a story of someone that they knew who had sadly lost their battle to cancer. Others would tell me that I am the strongest person they know, and that if anyone is going to beat it, that I would. Others said sorry, like they would when giving condolences to my immediate family at my impending funeral. Then others didn't know what to say or do and so said and did nothing at all. These first reactions may sound shocking and inconsiderate. However, everyone did the best they could with the life experiences that they have had right up until that moment, and so that first reaction was all they knew how to do. I genuinely wasn't emotionally affected by any of those reactions. I took away the aspects of those I needed and let the other words wash over me, like water off a duck's back.

The reactions and responses that seemed to impact me the most were possibly the simplest, really. They were from those who reached out to give me an embodying heartfelt hug, delivering comforting words like, "WE will get through this," "You are going to be okay," and "What can I do right now to support you?" There isn't anything extraordinary about these words; however, hearing them made all the difference to me. I didn't feel like I was doing this on my own. It made me feel like I could breathe that little bit easier. I may not have known exactly what I needed right in that moment, but I knew that down the line, when I did, I could confidently reach out and ask for the support I needed. Let me tell you briefly, by fast forwarding to some of those times when I did know. It sure was a roller coaster of diverse needs. They ranged from needing someone to cry with, to needing someone to cook my daughter and me healthy meals, someone to drive me to and from my chemotherapy and specialists appointments, someone to do my grocery shopping, someone to laugh with, walk with, sit with, and everything else in between. Mind you, that could have all been in the space of a single day.

What I learned from all the first reactions was that my recovery journey was not just about me. It was also about everyone in my life, every person that had crossed my path in order to provide me with what I needed to overcome, to heal, to thrive, and then to share with others what I had discovered and learnt along the way. Having cancer is NOT a death sentence. It's actually an enormous wake-up call. By sharing my experience, I hope that the person reading these words will not wait for a significant trauma or a diagnosis in their lives to take responsibility to start living their best life. I hope that they take that first step, however big or small, in creating an experience that they truly love and are proud to be living, that they find deep gratitude in each waking minute regardless of what that day may bring. I hope that they commit to taking action today, from this very moment, because we only ever have this exact moment to live. What we choose to do with it is entirely up to us. A series of single moments strung together will create what we look back on and call our lives. If you were to take a look back on all the moments you have lived up until now, would you be happy? If you answered yes, then good on you. Rock on! Keep doing what you are doing, and enjoy every moment that is yet to come.

However, if you answered no, then this is your chance to do something different, something completely and uncomfortably new.

Once the gravity of that message landed for me, it created such a significant shift in my thinking. I was no longer going to sit back and wait for life to come to me; I was going to go out and grab life by the proverbial horns! If you've been waiting for some kind of sign telling you it's time to start living life differently, then this is it! There's no better time than right NOW!

It became important to show family and friends that there can be a different outcome to what they had previously experienced. I was grateful for the lesson of not judging someone for their first reaction—if they knew differently, then they would do differently. Getting a swift kick up the backside from the universe was exactly what I needed to stop taking time for granted, and to start doing all of the things on my to-do list now! I have said yes to things that made me feel uncomfortable, and I will continue to do so daily, as it continues to support my growth as a human being. As Mary Engelbrite so beautifully said, "If you don't like something, change it. If you can't change it, then change the way you think about it."

I vividly remember the full-body response I had during a conversation with my good friend Linda. She said, "From the moment we are born, we are slowly dying." I remember my initial reaction was to question what she had said. Instead I sat back and allowed the words to sit in the pit of my stomach and to percolate, just like I would with coffee. The words jumped around my head, some landing comfortably, and then others being plucked back for further analysis. Finally, after what felt like hours, the words made sense to me. I knew from my studies that words only hold the meaning and energy that we give them. These words had now given me a new meaning and energy, specifically concerning this sacred opportunity we call 'life.' Technically, each and every day that we are alive brings us closer to the day we die. I know, it has some heaviness to it. Shouldn't knowing this mean that we choose to live each day of our lives more carefully? Should it not be filled with more joy, more contentment, and more gratitude? In my opinion, of course it should!

Remember earlier when I said that words hold energy and meaning? Well, I decided that I was not going to give the word 'cancer' any meaning in my life. I literally removed the word from my vocabulary. Instead I would refer to the tumor in my breast as, 'some confused cells.' Each time I was in a position to share my news with someone, I would lightheartedly say, "Yep, I'm just getting these confused cells sorted." That's all they were in my mind: cells that got the formula wrong when they duplicated. And so, in order for these confused cells to get clarity in my body, to get back to replicating using the healthy formula; my whole body, mind, and spirit had to first realign itself and find that exact same clarity.

I was particular about the words I chose to use in relation to my treatments. I would never use words like 'toxic' or 'poison' when referring to chemotherapy. Instead I would refer to it as the elixir of life. Some of the nurses smiled, because they just knew, and then others looked at me strangely. It didn't bother me either way. My body knew what it needed to thrive. At the hospital, I found my allocated day chair, that I eloquently dubbed my 'Queen' chair, popped the hands-free ear buds in my ears, and listened to my calming meditation while the 'elixir of life' worked its magic. This all played such a significant role in how my body received the treatment and how quickly I recovered. If I hadn't lost my hair, most people would be clueless to the fact I was going through a 'confused cells' treatment regime.

At home, this was the time I found power in stillness. Before my diagnosis, I was constantly busy, forever on the go. Then, all of a sudden, I had to be still. Everything other than my wellness was put on hold. Other than appointments, I had the four walls of my home to surround me, day in, day out. I recreated the vision I had of my home. I saw it as my own private sanctuary, a place where I could be whole and contentedly still. Sitting in my garden almost felt like I was being transported to one of the magnificent gardens in Kyoto, Japan. It was my special place; I would sit and listen to the bees buzzing amongst the bottle brush, just over my bamboo fence. I would single out the sounds of the birds singing to each other. I would watch the delicate, white butterflies flutter by and get swept up in small pockets of a quickening breeze, only to realize that their wings are actually quite strong. I'd sit and meditate and listen out for each new sound that would tantalize my senses. It is the space in which I feel safe, nurtured, and completely and unconditionally loved.

Finding harmony and balance outside of me encourages the harmony and balance within me. When I practiced this more, it triggered an interchangeable cycle. The easiest place I've consistently found harmony and balance has been in nature.

When I changed the energy in the language I used, from 'cancer' to 'confused cells,' it also changed the physiology of how my body responded to everything and everyone. Then in turn how everything and everyone responded to me, and the way that they saw my wellbeing. My gratitude came from knowing that I had complete control of how I responded to words and my environment. Dr. Joe Dispenza said, "If I master myself, then I can master my life." I will keep practicing this daily.

Living through a sibling's diagnosis and treatment, regardless of how intimately involved in the process, was very different from having lived the experience first-hand. It's so much easier to arrive at a logical conclusion or outcome when it's not your life that is being immediately impacted. The heaviness felt even more intense, because at the time of my diagnosis, I was a single parent to my daughter, Caira Juliet (CJ). It made sense that I not only made decisions that felt right for me, but also that through the process, I kept CJ in the forefront of my mind. I considered the impact and gravity of my decisions on her immediately and in the future.

I had two very different experiences to reflect upon with both my sisters' diagnoses. This example of gratitude was a very bittersweet one for me. I had the advantage (if you can call it that) of drawing from what worked and what didn't work for my sisters and then picking and choosing what I felt was right for me going forward. My parents were so amazing. Mum became my chef, my housekeeper, and mine and my daughter's caretaker when I was too physically fatigued to look after CJ myself. I know it gave her a sense of purpose, so she took on this role with passion and enthusiasm. If Mum saw that I was feeling well, that would absolutely make her day. My Dad was the provider, the grocery shopper, the handyman, and taxi driver when I needed him to be. Dad made sure that CJ still had some normality in her days to enjoy being a 9-year-old and not feel burdened by what was happening at home. They allowed me to entirely focus on myself and my healing because I had complete trust and confidence in them to look after my precious daughter.

My heart broke the day my parents had to bury their daughter, my sister Susy. No parent should ever have to go through that. It's not how life is meant to play out. So, it's no wonder that they did all they could to ensure I had everything I needed to get well and make a full recovery. There were times when they would question my decision on treatment plans. I understand their concerns came from a place of fear because of what they had already lived through with my sister. However, I reassured them that I would base all of my decisions on the full gamut of support available to me: my professional medical team, my reflexologist, my Reiki healer, my energy healer, my herbalist, and finally the one thing that would have me sitting in my 'neutral' space. Some call it intuition; I call it my 'neutral' space. It's that feeling I get in the pit of my stomach when I ask a question. There is no excitement. There is no nervousness—there is only calm, that neutral feeling. That's when I know I can trust my intuition, my 'neutral' space, as my go-to tool, to guide me each time I need to make a decision.

I found that when I use past experiences to make decisions for my life going forward, I need to make absolutely sure that those decisions are based on a feeling derived from love and not from fear. I trust that I know what is best for me and my wellbeing. When I tap into that 'neutral' feeling, I am grateful because I know that I am on the right track.

After my bi-lateral mastectomy and reconstructive surgery, all I was focused on was recovering, getting well and staying well. The last thing on my mind was going out and looking for a romantic partner. After all, my body was different. It didn't look or feel the same as it did before. It was going to take some time to accept that this new body was what I had to work with for the rest of my life. So, sure, I found the silver lining in having new fabricated breasts by saying that I would have the perkiest ones in the nursing home when I finally got there in my old age. Annnd… that I finally got the correct size breasts I should have always had, except I went about it in a very convoluted way. A year post reconstructive surgery recovery, I was getting used to my shapely 'lovely lady lumps.' I was finding comfort in my new body, even seeing glimmers of confidence peeking through.

My beautiful mother, bless her, took it upon herself to bring the old tradition of matchmaking back into the modern world. Clearly in her mind, I had not done such a great job of finding myself a decent suitor in the past, so she handed me a business card of a business manager she'd met when purchasing a car. I still don't know what it was that made me trust my mother's judgement on this, but I did.

Our first meeting, the blind date, was an absolute success. It was such a pleasant surprise. John made me laugh a lot. He listened intently to what I had to say. During our conversation, I found him to be kind and generous, and he carried strong family values. So we hit it off right away. It's been a few years since that first date now. However, it has led to a rewarding and fulfilling relationship. John supports me in all that I do. He is someone I can rely on, and he encourages me to reach for the stars. I trust him. He has embraced all of me; he holds me in my vulnerability and gently kisses my tears. He sees past the health challenges I face, as he has only ever looked at me through his vision of me being full of life, health, and vitality. I am so grateful that my Mother had the courage to start that conversation with John, and that I took the leap of faith and said yes to the opportunity that had presented itself to me.

When I learned to accept all of my scars as a unique story piece being added to my life's tapestry, I learned to genuinely love all of me, especially my imperfections. I am grateful for this lesson as it opened the door of opportunity for somebody to enter my life, somebody to love me unconditionally. I thought that cliché saying by the quirky Lucille Ball, "Love yourself first, and everything else falls in line," was a crock. However, it turns out it was right on point!

My journey to wellness hasn't always been rosy though. There were many days when my body ached all over. The pins and needles in my hands and feet were too much to bear. Losing my taste buds because of chemo meant I often had no appetite. It was all tasteless when I did eat, anyway. I could have quite easily stayed in bed for the full week between my treatments and appointments.

I couldn't though. I needed to find something, just one thing that would give me the motivation to keep going, keep getting out of bed, to keep showing up so that my body got everything it needed to heal and thrive. Some people find that one thing in their faith, others find it in their sport. I found it in my daughter, CJ. She is the light at the end of the tunnel. When fear crept in, I thought of her. When it felt like my world had completely turned upside down and inside out, she was the beacon of light guiding me back onto my path. Her sheer existence demanded that I be present to her, interact with her, protect her, nurture her, and teach her young, impressionable self. After all, this was the promise I made to her when she was in utero.

I am a firm believer in walking my talk, in demonstrating my values and the attributes that I find endearing so that my daughter can experience what I find important in life. I don't expect her to have the same values as I do. She is her own person with her own life experiences. I just want her to be resilient and be able to tackle adversity head on when it comes her way. Over these past few years, I have enjoyed watching CJ grow into a beautiful, compassionate, intelligent, strong willed, and creative young woman.

I am eternally grateful that I had the experience of conceiving and carrying CJ to full term, of raising her on my own and sharing this life with her. I feel like I have been awarded the highest of honors. CJ is and always will be my life's greatest achievement.

Mahatma Gandhi said it perfectly: "Be the change you want to see in the world." I completely embody that, as my daily choices influence how CJ sees the world, and how she will eventually show up as an adult. Demonstrating the attitude of gratitude to CJ, especially through some of the darkest of times, was vital.

I feel fortunate to have had a head start in practicing gratitude as a life tool. Having had the opportunity to reflect on my own life experiences and immerse myself in many years of personal development has helped me refine my gratitude towards everything that comes into my experience.

I find gratitude in listening to a song that lifts my spirit;
I find gratitude in having a conversation with a loved one;

I find gratitude in eating nutritional meals;
I find gratitude in hearing my daughter's laughter;
I find gratitude in escorting a spider back outside;
I find gratitude in giving a random stranger a lovely compliment.

And so much more. However, this is my list of gratitude. Remember when I asked earlier, "If you were to take a look back on all of the moments you have lived up until now, would you be happy?" Regardless what you answered earlier, if you are ready to start practicing the attitude of gratitude and want a simple way, then here it is:

Buy a notebook. For the next 30 days, spend at least ten minutes each evening reflecting on the day. Write down three to five things, beginning each line with 'Today, I am grateful for... ' and finish the sentence with what you were grateful for. Then—this is the important part—read the list out loud to yourself, so that the words' vibration solidifies from thought into matter. As a bonus, ask a loved one what they were grateful for in their day, and start a conversation that will create a ripple effect of the beauty that is the attitude of gratitude.

My final lesson is that no matter what life throws at you, finding gratitude in everyday experiences is what ultimately brings joy to life. Although my cancer diagnosis deeply redefined my attitude of gratitude, there is no need to wait for something as traumatic as this to be shaken up and realize that there are so many things, big and small, to appreciate. In learning all these profound lessons, I can now wholeheartedly say I honestly believe that there is always something to be grateful for.

I'm not completely out of the woods just yet. I don't know how long I will walk this life path, but what I can say is that I have done my absolute best to live a hundred lifetimes within the last four years. I have squeezed every last drop out of my days and nights. From every person who has crossed my path, to every unique experience I have had, every meal I have tasted, every sunshine that has warmed my face, every destination I have had the pleasure of visiting, and all the opportunities I have embraced—I have found a piece of gratitude in it all.

Right now, I am living my best life; I have everything I need. My garden sanctuary surrounds me, the sun is warming my face, the cherry blossoms are in bloom, I'm holding a freshly brewed cup of Rosehip tea, and my daughter's sweet laughter is playing in my ears. My heart is beaming with happiness and again, today, I am grateful.

Love and light, yesterday, today, and for always.

"Gratitude for the present moment and the fullness of life now is the true prosperity."

~ Eckhart Tolle

CHAPTER TEN

Shifting Your Focus to Gratefulness

By Joanne Singleton

W hen a crisis occurs, we have various attitude choices on how we can react to the situation. The keywords for me are 'attitude' and 'reaction.' Some events occur that are not within our control yet affect us momentously. The multi-faceted spectrum of different emotions come into play, many as we have experienced; it is the inevitable part of life. Negative emotions can create stress, anger, guilt, and heaviness in one's life, whereas positive feelings can bring faith, inspiration, happiness, and a clearer path for greater opportunities to come our way. Love softens, whereas fear hardens and creates isolation. To live life in gratitude, we need to shift our attitude towards gratefulness, even in the most challenging times. Consciously making a habitual choice to find and express appreciation in one's life, no matter how big or small, creates for much bluer skies ahead. Jogging our memory to how wonderful we feel when things go well and searching for that piece of goodness in all situations will help re-create that once loved feeling and guide us along the highway of happiness. There will always be peaks and valleys in life, but reminding ourselves that "this too shall pass" helps lighten the air we breathe.

A lesson is most often revealed in difficult times, making us stronger and ultimately more appreciative of the present moment. I always ask myself, *What am I supposed to learn from this?* Even when I initially think, *Absolutely nothing!,* something always pops up when I settle on having an open mind and then doing my best to approach the situation with love. It can be hard, but I continuously try to be objective. I stand back and look at the problem rather than dance in the chaos. When I'm thinking a million things, I know I've been dancing way too long. Being objective and observing from the outside helps create a clearer head for me to think things through and help shift my being to an attitude of appreciation and understanding. It is said that misery loves company, and I have certainly had my share of sharing or complaining too much. Passengers love to jump on that bus. Being thankful leaves room only for grateful passengers and, ultimately, a smoother ride for all.

When my mother passed away five years ago, after the numbness subsided, I remember thinking that I could either fold or pick myself up, dust myself off, and put one foot in front of the other. I had no idea where that next step would take me, but I knew it would help me move forward. I, and possibly others who have experienced profound loss, felt like I had a huge rug pulled out from underneath my feet, leaving me with absolutely nothing to hold onto. The stability and grounding had to come from within. My mom and I had an extremely close connection, and now I was flying solo. Someone once said to me that when this event happens, the umbilical cord would be cut, and I would have to start over. For me, this was quite an accurate way of putting it. He was right! As we all know, an umbilical cord is cut at birth, though the energy connection of the oneness we shared in our relationship remained, making the new journey with her tough. Along with that, the heart's physical pain was like something I had never experienced before. I now understand how people can actually die from a broken heart. My heart really hurt and did so for quite some time. So choosing to dust myself off, and with a lot of personal understanding, huge attitude adjustment, and faith for this new journey ahead without my best friend, I kept reminding myself of how grateful and blessed I was to have had this amazing woman as my mother and best friend. My attitude while grieving, choosing to be thankful, helped me heal. Along with my family and friends' love, we bridged the gap of sadness to a grander appreciation for everything I looked at, experienced, and wanted. In the blink of an eye, it's true: your life can change. Mom always said, "Be thankful

you are breathing another day," "Never settle for seconds," and
heaven or hell to her was right where she stood. "Share your life
with those who make you smile, and as for the others, walk away,
but do it graciously." Not a day goes by that I don't think about my
mom or miss her dearly, but her spirit was so full and her love,
unconditional; she always wanted me to smile. I know she is still
with me. She leaves me dimes in the oddest places, even when
traveling, and always on special days. In tough times, when I see
that dime, I smile and carry on, knowing that all is going to be
okay. Of course, I pick them up. I've saved many. No matter the
adverse event, our attitude of how we react will determine if the
doors of life will open or close; whichever one we choose, it is our
choice, no one else's. You are the producer and director of your
life, so create an amazing script. Was the deep connection with my
mom and the ultimate heartbreak worth it? You bet it was! Always,
always choose love.

Recently, as we have come to know all too well, COVID-19 has
thrown the world a massive curveball. It is incredible how the
spinning globe of uncertainty and confusion can travel through
one's mind, experiencing fear and devastation like never before,
but also for some, shifting to sweeping away the clutter and debris,
leaving space for clarity, lightness, tranquility, and gratitude. With
the ever-changing decisions on how we are supposed to live or not
supposed to live, this pandemic seems to be more "real" than one
could have imagined. It has tremendously changed peoples'
lifestyles, personally and professionally, some due to order, choice,
and unfortunate circumstances. These changes have also left others
with time for self-internalization and reconnection with their souls,
while others are walking in circles, not knowing where to go or
when to stop. Everyone's personal views and reactions to the
consequences of the virus can be completely different, possibly
because of direct effect, beliefs, learned behavior, or simply the
grandness of uncertainty. We haven't done this before, not to this
extent. Many people have become more mindful of their neighbors
and strangers, realizing how one's individual act can react like a
deck of cards having a positive domino effect. The opposite has
held true for some, and unfortunately, that deck of cards resulted in

not so good a hand. Again, finding a speck of gratefulness benefits significantly and has rewarding returns. What we give, we get! Our attitude is a choice, so we should choose wisely.

With self-isolation and social distancing becoming the new way of life, mingling with our families, friends, and colleagues has become very limited, creating loneliness, boredom, stir-crazy feelings, depression, and anxiety. Through this raw, emotional non-choice of being by oneself or isolated with family, creativity and inspiration have blossomed, hearts have been renewed, judgments and unnecessary opinions have eased, and the doors once believed to have been sealed shut from opportunity or growth have now squeaked open. This is definitely a double-edged sword, with each side's goal being to become equally blunt, some cradled with love, understanding, empathy, and compassion, and some with more anger, anxiety, fear, and bewilderment. These raw emotions, attitudes of appreciation, and gratification for the new adventures being discovered have also watered the soul's seed to reawaken the heart, painting a new life picture.

Our essential global services have remained on guard, placing momentous risks to their personal lives, only to save others' lives. The truest of heroes are every one of them; "Thank you, thank you, thank you" only tips the iceberg of gratitude for these angels on earth. We have been silenced in this chaotic existence, eventually leaving vast room to wade through the snowstorm that has affected every person on our planet. Many gaps have also been unusually bridged in relationships, birthing an intimate human element operating deep from within. The grudges once held seem to fade more easily and our tenderness has been renewed. Like the seed of a flower working its way up through the soil to reach the sunlight's magnetization, we, too, are growing and opening up. In silence, we blossom.

With our world being turned upside down, inside out, and thrown out the other side, we have learned to remain connected to others via social media, technology, telephone calls, or the good old-fashioned way of writing a letter or sending a personal note. Some people have had to literally learn how to operate and navigate a computer from scratch. And, for high-tech individuals, they have become experts on a much larger scale. We all continue to learn something. Much of our technological world, which I once believed had taken away our personal connections to one another, has become the new norm, but I now choose to see it with a unique, special flare. When we cannot touch, hold, or hug, through no choice of our own, we have explored and improvised in a meaningful way. We have either built or solidified our relationships from afar with our new way of living. This unique style has shaped a greater appreciation for the loved ones we were once able to spend time with whenever we chose, to the heartfelt excitement to the ones we are waiting to hug for the first time. Many have opened themselves up to new friendships and opportunities, personally and professionally, creating new space in their lives for a richer, more deeply satisfying experience. Countless are very grateful for all these new opportunities that have sprung and may not have arisen otherwise.

In speaking with my friends over coffee from afar, we have most certainly concluded that a clear shift has taken place in our lives on many levels. Some are swallowing the peacefulness settled at heart, while others feel like an engine sitting idle at a red light, but the light had turned green and your foot remains on the brake because of the rules in place. With the multitude of restrictions from public and government sectors being forced upon us, dictating how we are required to live, a space of clarity eventually appeared. The sounds of the honking horns got louder and louder—the honks of the soul. Having so much time by yourself, you begin to turn within. For many, gas pedals were accelerated, taking a leap of faith on an unknown adventure with only hope and trust in their suitcase of life. Downright scary, with bravery blended in… so much has truly changed.

While out for my walks in the early morning, afternoon, or evening hours the neighborhood presented a vast space of stillness and peacefulness to its vacant streets. Only left to be shared were the sounds of nature at your side. Listening to the rushing of the creek's rapid flowing water traveling over rocks and debris, to the singing from the birds in the nearby trees, all without the hustle and bustle of traffic passing by, provided a deeper awareness and appreciation for all whom we share our space with. Birds actually chirp quite loudly when talking to one another, and their melodies are beautiful. It is so sweet to hear the early morning chirps of the baby birds calling out for their parents when they have gone in search of breakfast, and their parents' response letting them know they are nearby. The communication between the different species of birds, including their existence with the other little creatures alongside them, is quite astounding.

Being a viewer to their active lives was like watching a nature show undisturbed. With the extra time on our hands, stronger friendships with the crows who visit our yard have developed. A deeper trust between them and us has equally been earned. The family arrives on our deck no later than 8:00 am to collect the breakfast that we have offered. The mom and dad have introduced their three babies, and all feel safe and welcome. Crows are extremely intelligent, and once trust is earned, they feel very comfortable—comfortable enough to fly under our cabana while sitting on the outdoor patio furniture. This friendly soul swoops in, touching the top of my head and then continues on his or her flight path. Their claws are quite sharp. I believe it's the mom letting me know that the family is hungry. I will refer to this little friend as "she" in my story as I've seen her feed her babies. When I was gardening the other evening, I was bent over picking the weeds, and she flew by me three times, touching my back, taking off and landing on the post nearby and then intently staring at me. It was clear my attention was being sought. We had to have a little talk, because she really didn't need to do that as often as she did. The most memorable experience was when I was on my deck gardening with my back turned from my doorway and when I turned around, this little critter was casually walking out from our house. I couldn't believe it. She also likes to stand at the open door from the deck, hop into the house a bit, and then I have to tell her that she must be outside. She then turns around and out she hops as if she understands what I am saying. When I arrive home from

146

work, she either flies to the roof of my car, or when I open the door and turn around to reach in for my purse, this little friend sits on my open door. It's dinner time.

Strange, to say the least... or is it? The family feels very comfortable in our space, and we clearly feel the same way. There is a grand awareness of realization that we share, side-by-side and intertwined, in this beautiful place we call earth that we share with other living creatures. This given time has created a deeper level of respect and a profound appreciation for and understanding of the connection that we uniquely have with all living species. Respect, peace, and stillness created an invisible bridge to one another. I also see this as the attitude that we chose to make known towards our counterparts that made all the difference in the world. We could have shooed our little friends away, creating stress and chaos, and possibly hurt feelings. Had we not appreciated or welcomed our new friends, we would have lost out on this unique, enduring friendship that developed.

Being grateful amidst a pandemic can be extremely challenging at the best of times, as many have experienced. Every emotion possible is displayed on the sleeves of millions, and the global disruption is extremely difficult to comprehend. In one way or another, COVID-19 has touched us all, threading every one of us more tightly into the tapestry of human existence—one quilt, millions of threads.

Every moment in our life is a new experience to savor, and carrying an attitude of gratitude keeps you connected to your soul and purpose in life. In the busyness of life, we can easily get sidetracked, but when we reconnect with ourselves, we feel the words, "Well, hello there. I've been patiently waiting for you." When that reconnection happens, all lights go on like an internal fireworks celebration. This feeling creates a fantastic sense of stability, clearness, and contentment, with an awareness that your path has become much smoother. Once this reconnection is experienced, it is almost impossible to turn back or ignore, just like when we accept the truth. Arguing with yourself is the worst argument you can have, and it's a guaranteed loss. Your newfound gratitude created by your attitude shines the light for your once-clouded walkway, which can happen when we forget about ourselves. Imagine how Dorothy felt in *The Wizard of Oz* when she clicked her heels together three times and said, "There's no place like home." Having a sense of wholeness helps in dealing with whatever comes your way.

Yourdictionary.com's definition of attitude is "a way of feeling or acting toward a person, thing, or situation." Finding gratitude in every situation can be challenging, but consciously stopping yourself and digging deep to find even a speck of gratitude can encourage a new thinking pattern resulting in a happier outlook. Happiness, I believe, comes from within, and reconnecting with the soul is a starting point to a road of tremendous joy. Being grateful for "*you*" literally puts a smile on your face and warms the heart. Your attitude transforms from the fullness, or lack thereof, that you experience within yourself, then portray to the outside world, and that ultimately gets magnetized back to you. What goes around, comes around. Feeling good on the inside makes everything look and feel a little bit brighter. It's incredible how one internal act can flood a multitude of returned joy. It's all in the way we look at and react to things. A simple smile can turn someone's life around. A human-to-human positive-energy gesture does wonders without a spoken word, and it doesn't cost a penny!

During Phase I of the COVID-19 pandemic, I was still going into the office, practicing self-distancing with all safety measures in place. When driving to work, the roads were barren. Vacant space on the once busied highway felt incredibly odd. I specifically remember one bright morning, driving down the highway with only a few other cars on the road, one being an ambulance. I drove past, honked my horn, and waved, and was immediately waved back at by the ambulance personnel. All of a sudden, goosebumps filled my body and I became quite emotional. The tears streamed down my cheeks and I felt a very heartful connection to strangers who help our community without giving it a second thought. My appreciation for them was overwhelming.

I continued on my way to work and when I was about to turn left on the road close to my underground parking, a bus had stopped allowing me to do so. Eye contact was reached with this lovely bus driver no more than 30 years old, I'm guessing. We smiled at each other he had the cutest dimples and again, a connection was made with only a smile and meeting eye to eye. A profound connection of knowing we are all in this together, walking the same path of uncertainty and fear, but doing it together... it was extremely powerful. Nothing existed for that moment except our smiles at each other. The stillness, quietness, and vacantness created by this life-altering event enabled this to happen. It was quite the morning, and I am forever grateful for those two unusual experiences. Through these encounters, I began to feel more open to people and the connections we have on an unspoken level.

After that, I consciously decided to interact with more people, which has since served me very well with the new people who have come into my life. Open the doors to your heart, and it's amazing what can happen. My gratitude attitude created a unique space within myself to enjoy my life at a deeper level, putting many more smiles on faces and feeling more open to the possibilities in life.

Though few of us team members arrived at the office daily, I felt that a deeper level of trust, compassion, and friendship developed with them. We were clearly in this dilemma together, and our attitudes for the respect we had for one another shined through in our interactions and concerns for each other. Our positive attitudes had an immense impact on remaining to provide the utmost care and compassion for our clients, ensuring that their needs were met and doing our best to relieve any fear or worry. We operated like family in every sense of the word. Through this grave uncertainty, I found that we somehow laughed more, shared more, and seemed to accomplish more than before. Our attitudes on how we responded to the ever-changing times played a significant role in getting through this. If someone wasn't having the best day, we helped turn that feeling around by listening and sharing our feelings, combined with light-heartedness and laughter. It was a choice, and we made a conscious effort to make each day a happy day. It was unspoken on many occasions, simply just shown in the way we treated one another.

Gratitude for life-long friendships grew even more profound. Not being able to see each other created a new fast-track bridge to each other. You would think you would know everything about someone whom you've known for over 50 years. Well, when there is extra time on your hands, many newfound bits and pieces come to light, cementing our friendship even deeper from what we knew to be already cemented firmly in place. This made it clear that there is always room for discovery and growth. We continued chatting on the phone, often more than once daily, and we continued to listen and support each other without judgment, to cry when needed and to laugh from deep within our bellies, sometimes to the point of crying, when it's way too hard to stop, even after the call was over. How many friends do you have who would answer their phone at 2:00 am if you called? I hope that you have many or at least one. My dear friend would, and I am forever grateful for this deepened friendship and would do the same for her in a heartbeat. Who said sisters had to only be by blood? Well, I think it was in Grade 4 that we became blood sisters, when that was the thing to do back then. I also know that my amazing children, who I am forever blessed and eternally grateful for, would answer their phones late into the night. I sleep every night with my phone by my side, volume high.

With friends, we've talked at great lengths about bringing the "attitude of gratitude" into our day, no matter if a good, bad, or indifferent experience presented itself. With each situation, we encourage each other to find some blessings or lessons. It can be more than difficult at times, but with the reminder that our attitude is the basis for our response, finding even a tidbit of appreciation helps achieve a more positive outcome, more precise understanding, and lightness. I believe that there is a reason for everything, and for every person that enters our lives. We sometimes have to go with the flow to see where we are to be, making sure we keep our eyes open to the forks in the road to choose which one to take. It is said that those forks can easily be missed. The fork has four tines, and if it takes more than one tine to make it right for you, so be it. If it takes more forks, so be it, too. Life is a journey. I believe that there is love in each experience, and remembering how good something felt and how grateful you are for that helps bring that feeling back into your day, no matter what is going on. These wedges of heartfelt feelings in your chest are much more durable than the heaviness sometimes felt. Keep reliving those feelings of the beautiful wedges experienced and they will grow, as love holds the greatest power. From here, it clears a pathway to walk daily in gratitude.

I genuinely believe we owe it to ourselves, each other, and the future souls yet to join us to do our best to walk this journey together, supporting each other with the human kindness we were gifted at birth and being kind to ourselves, first and foremost. Though we will carry on with our busy lives, I will try not to let life get in the way of what's important. Please join me.

As I close this chapter, writing in my dark, quiet office late at night, I am deeply grateful to have had this opportunity to share a piece of me with you.

"Gratitude opens the door to
the power, the wisdom,
the creativity of the
universe. You open
the door through gratitude."

~ Deepak Chopra

CHAPTER ELEVEN

EMBRACING THE GIFT

By Anup Batra

In 1992, when I had just turned twenty-one, I started sailing on the high seas as the youngest Marine Engineer from my batch. I had many exciting life experiences, including visiting festive port cities with dazzling nightlife, sailing through cyclonic storms in rough seas, and even an encounter with armed pirates who wanted to capture our ship. Especially notable was an experience when my ship sailed through a very harsh storm in the South China Sea. It was remarkable how our team of deck officers, engineers, and crew got together to face the challenge under the captain's leadership. Our captain, who was a very experienced seaman and an outstanding person, did not catch a wink for 90 hours straight.

During this time of crisis, when our ship was sailing through the cyclone, my marine officers and engineers showed a lot of kindness for the junior staff, and they asked us to rest in our cabins. We felt a deep sense of gratitude for the seniors and instead decided to give them a helping hand. Each one of us prayed and put in our best efforts during that time of hardship. Despite all of the rolling and pitching through the roughest cyclone, we managed to get into calm waters and finally land in a port of China. When we finally landed, there was a sense of jubilation, a sense of togetherness for what we had achieved in unity. We felt very grateful to each other for delivering a higher standard.

Sailing has brought so much appreciation and many life lessons into my reality. When I was sailing on the Pacific in the high seas in 1996, we came to Wollongong in Australia. I was permitted by my senior engineer to go ashore and see the port. I was very excited about it. I went and explored the place and interacted with the Australian people. I found them to be remarkable in how they greeted visitors from a foreign land. I was welcomed to many different places. For instance, I was invited to a community club where several native people offered me a beer and asked me to visit their homes and farms. I had come to Australia after sailing in 27 countries, and I felt like I understood these people. They know how to live life. I knew that, sometime in life, I would like to come back here and live with them.

I stopped sailing in 1997, and after my last voyage, I went into the corporate sector. Seven years later, in 2004, just when I needed a fresh start in life, I got an opportunity to migrate to Australia. This opportunity came to me just as I had gone to visit an Indian-Australian forum and was offered a chance to see the country to study and work. As a new immigrant, there were a series of challenges that I had to face. I had come to join an MBA program at Monash University, and I realized how expensive it could be to live in Australia. Life here was difficult for a student. It was hard to pay the university fees and also manage all of the other personal expenses.

So, after I came to Australia, I thought that I probably would not sustain myself. I thought that I'd go back to India, but very surprisingly, the Monash University conducted a scholarship exam. And the very next day, I got an email from the vice-chancellor saying that I had been selected for a scholarship, so I would not have to pay fees. That was a significant milestone in my life because I realized that the universe is willing to give us whatever we need. We have to have faith in it. I experienced sincere gratitude, because I am not alone; the universe is always by my side.

This feeling of alignment with the spirit opened up a whole new world for me.

I decided to stay in Australia. And even after the scholarship, I had a tough journey ahead finding a job for myself. Initially, I started offering tuitions to junior students during this time and carried on with my cash expenditure. I eventually managed to find a fascinating job as a business development manager with a company that offered me a meager base salary. The upside of that job was that they offered to share with me a substantial percentage of the recurring revenue, which would be earned due to my efforts.

I did not look down on the opportunity because they paid me a low hourly rate; instead, I felt gratitude that they were willing to share revenue. I accepted the job offer immediately. I gave it my absolute commitment and directly landed a few major clients. The senior management was astounded by my performance and started sending fresh opportunities my way. Because I always had a thankful heart, I considered the job to be a gift and felt like I had to reciprocate it by growing the company. I worked with relentless effort and a winning spirit.

So, let's go back a bit and talk about the initial challenge, which faced me when I was offered a low hourly rate. What was the attitude and thought process that inspired me to take it on? I focused on the opportunity to succeed and to be on a journey to riches. But for that, I had to generate new business without wasting any time. I felt that if I had faith and left no stone unturned, I would attract the right clients for the company and achieve results that would enrich me. People were receptive to my ideas because they could sense my attitude. I ended up creating strong relationships with the decision makers in the client companies, thus creating healthy relationships with our client base.

At this time, I was in a situation where I was challenged to prove myself. That voice was so loud that everything else became irrelevant. There were naysayers everywhere. Some people were coming in and saying that I should not have taken on this job with better jobs available to me. Some said that the business owners were unnecessarily manipulating me. Still, I came more from a sense of gratitude, as I felt that they had allowed me to generate revenue for them, as well as generate income for myself and improve my standard in life. I approached the opportunity from that positive perspective. I felt like the universe responded to my attitude. And one client after the other started coming on board.

Even though finding a job as a new immigrant was hard, this company gave me the opportunity.

The first decision was to accept the offer. I took the job. Then I set forth to make the most of it.

The second decision was to be very focused and not listen to so many different people who tried to advise me. Instead, I chose to follow the direction of my inner compass, which intuitively knew the answers. Another business development manager was working in the same role as me but had minimal success, even though he was highly skilled and experienced. He went against himself because he used to waste his energy complaining about senior management and business directors. I felt that he was attracting negative energy as a result of this behavior. And he was quite relaxed about how he went through the day. As for me, every minute was urgent, and I managed to maximize my time. I maximized opportunities every hour. I set a goal to work nonstop until I had generated an opening in the morning, then have a break while feeling the satisfaction of work well done, and then resume my momentum.

I achieved success much faster than others. Because of being thankful for the opportunity, I put in massive effort to honor the company. I always felt that if they put the trust in me, then I should come from a place of giving back to them by helping to make the company successful.

After that, I made some critical decisions about creating a balance in life so that I was not just looking after my financial responsibilities. Still, I was also making sure that my studies were going well. The university was quite demanding. There were lots of assignments and group work to be done. There were classes to attend. I changed my courses to evening classes to do my job during the day and attend classes in the evening. Then I did my assignments at night. And sometimes I took time off from my job and met up with my group mates to do our assignments. So, it was a juggling act by which I was trying to balance multiple responsibilities. But I noticed that everyone understood what I was doing, and they were very cooperative and helped me succeed.

There were challenges along the way and I had to make some firm decisions to overcome them. One day, my boss, a director of the company, asked me to become full-time with the firm and reduce my university hours. I had to think about that one. But I decided to go full-time. I lowered my university hours, went full-time with the company, and applied for my permanent resident visa in Australia. The company offered to get me a visa, which would allow me to work full-time. I went along with them, and, eventually, I got full-time work rights. That allowed me to double my commitment at work and help to grow that company. My core values and beliefs guided this decision.

One of the beliefs I've always had in life is to embrace the opportunity, even if it means that I have to stretch myself to make the most of what life is offering. My belief system also includes having that sense of gratitude for people who create these opportunities for me and to make sure that I never disappoint them and never let them down when they extend themselves to me.

Whether it's a client investing in a company or an employer investing in an employee, they are forthcoming in either case. So, that's where a sense of gratitude helps instead of having a sense of expectation or entitlement. If we come from a place of appreciation and gratitude, the universe opens up doors for us because the energy of appreciation syncs with the positive life force of the world, which automatically opens new doors and opportunities in our lives.

After I decided to help grow the company that had given me such a great opportunity, I felt like I had renewed energy to do so and, within three years, I managed to increase it by about 250%. The leadership team was grateful to me. By that time, I had created the company's systems and capabilities and recruited new staff and mentored them. And if I needed to do so, I could leave them on that path and start my own business. Eventually, in 2007, I started my own business in Australia, which I'm still running. I put 110%

commitment into my business and worked to acquire skills, both in business development and on a leadership level, which I use consistently to coach new people and achieve desirable outcomes for my business. One of the main lessons that I have learned is that we should be grateful to everyone, whether it's a supplier, an employee, or a client. We should always come from an open heart with a sense of gratitude.

Fast forward 15 years to today. I have been running my own business for more than a decade.

We are all going through a pandemic. It threw us off entirely, setting us back by four months. It came suddenly, and all of our clients started calling us and canceling their contracts or putting them on hold. Our revenue went down to almost 20% of what it was. At one point, 80% of our revenue was wiped out within three days and it felt like maybe now, there would be no business at all, but I've always acted with the belief that whenever there is some adversity, it carries a gift with it. We just need an attitude of gratitude, and life makes us see the seeds of something new when something else is lost.

I went with that belief and decided to give it a hundred percent and make my business work. I never let any staff members feel like things would not happen. This was my time to act like the captain of the ship. And I acted upon my self-belief; I gave confidence to every member of my team. All of them were in it with me to make things happen. We strengthened our marketing message and we increased our business development process. We also came up with innovation and focus.

We discovered that digital technology businesses were still thriving at a time when a lot of other businesses were not able to. While marketing itself may be put on hold because businesses can't close sales, there were other opportunities a digital business could innovate and venture into. We decided to expand our services beyond marketing and include things like strategic capital raising because of the investment community.

We're still putting money into technology ventures, and technology ventures are hungry for capital. We decided to help them out in being investor-ready and obtaining capital, which gave them the fuel to grow their companies. We had networks from which potential clients could benefit. So, we added this new feature of finding strategic partnerships for our clients and helping companies enter new markets.

Among the many lessons that I've learned is we always have to deliver the very best that we can in any situation with an attitude of gratitude. This translates into goodwill from everywhere, because all people like to be appreciated and most people are never appreciated enough. So, when we are the ones who understand them, they are willing and ready to go the extra mile for us. Then we create positive energy and an environment in which even ordinary people deliver extraordinary results.

During the present time, I care for my state of mind. I always do meditation before I leave my house in the morning because I find that I stay connected to the higher self through meditation. That connection allows a sense of calm, gratitude, and good energy into my life. When I manage people, they are all inspired to follow me and go the extra mile to make things happen. I think that is a significant determinant of anyone's success. When the coronavirus occurred, we were thrown off course and were at 20% of our revenue. Even so, bit by bit, with the support of the team, we moved forward. And just last week, we exceeded pre-COVID figures, giving us a sense of stability and confidence in our future as a company.

For me, gratitude is really a very subtle thing. My need to feel grateful may be essential, like coming from that space of authenticity and connection to people. It creates good vibes and positive energy. But more than that, I do feel that it's also necessary to do tangible things to show appreciation for what people are doing. Sometimes I give someone a gift. If I know they've done some extraordinary work and enjoy wine, I will buy them a couple of bottles of their favorite wine. Or, if someone has put in extra effort, I might send them a handwritten note praising precisely what they have done. That's valuable. I make sure that I give them such a message from time to time. So, in my own life, I first and foremost keep acknowledging people, and I also recognize the universe.

For me, true gratitude starts with gratitude to the Almighty, because whatever we do, whatever we achieve is because of divine grace. If we connect to the higher power, we are naturally in a state of appreciation and gratitude and good vibes. That's why I always start my day with meditation, and I end my day with meditation. My practice is to spend ten minutes in meditation just before I go to sleep and as soon as I wake up. This meditation is an acknowledgment of the creator. My whole day becomes more infused with the divine connection, which creates a more soulful life in which I naturally appreciate people when they do something good.

As a result of having gratitude, I feel more aligned with the universe and more soulful. I have a better connection with people and am blessed with more prosperity, better health, and greater wealth in my life. Sometimes, I am in a deeply connected state. The universe automatically points me in the right direction. My intuition is stronger, and people around me are also displaying similar vibes. I create a happy environment around me.

Earlier in my life, I tried to do things almost by pushing and did not understand the universe's magnetic energy. Things sometimes got done, while at other times, there was frustration. I felt like I wasn't in flow and I wasn't able to achieve my goals. Now, I see myself in an inspired state when I visualize what I want to achieve—and then I attract it into my life.

When I began my spiritual connection and gratitude journey, I started getting more and more satisfaction from life. I explored the concept deeply. Many times, I was so happy to see the energy increase in places where I entered that, as a result, I acted as a leader.

With gratitude as a foundation, the energy also went from me to my team, friends, and family, but it came back from them as well. As a result, I do things effortlessly. That's a massive transformation in me; life is not about pushing or struggling to achieve anything. Life is about beingness. In life, actually, if you look at it, there are three things: Being, Doing, and Having, and most people focus on having, and I used to focus on this as well. I used to measure myself by how much I have in my life.

What have I achieved in my life? I was always obsessed with that. But now I've realized that it's all about beingness, because if we take care of our being, then the doing and having automatically take care of themselves.

As I savor my life lessons, I am in sincere gratitude for every experience that has enriched my life. I have a thirst for knowledge and an understanding of how life works and the more profound principles that shape our lives.

My first lesson in life was that the main thing that makes a difference in our quality of life is how we see things. It's not what happens to us but how we perceive what is happening. Whether we pass through a cyclone on the high seas or go through a pandemic, if we see the situation as a gift that will enrich us, we will allow a series of positive events to unfold. When we were experiencing the cyclone, the team acted with poise and mutual respect, bringing about a coordinated effort under a strong leader to overcome the situation.

The second lesson I learned is that intention has energy. If we have clarity, focus, and commitment, seemingly impossible events and goals start materializing. There is always a lot of noise around us. It is up to us whether we get drowned in these voices or maintain our focus and positivity. Everyone who impacts our lives is providing an opportunity for us to enrich ourselves. When that voice in our heads has negativity or when doubt comes up, we can replace it with our novel perspective of looking for the opportunity in the situation. In my current business, I am often confronted with situations for which I have no answers. The problem could be about projects, cash flow, clients, or the staff. I have always found that when I act from a position of gratitude and positivity, these situations change entirely and leave behind a gift to embrace. Life is full of circumstances that can be turned around with the right attitude.

The third lesson I learned is that practicing gratitude as a way of life changes our attitude towards everything and endows us with a positive vibe. This vibe emits and attracts positive energy and manifests the most treasured gifts in life. A practical way of doing this is to build conscious awareness of all the things that have been and are manifesting for us. Using a gratitude journal amplifies this process.

In summary, life is not what happens to us but what we make of it by the power of positive vision, clear intention, and appreciation of the small and big things that are happening for us at any moment. We can make this change at any time and start experiencing a richer life, both on the spiritual and material levels. Life is truly a celebration. Embrace the gift.

**"So much has been given to
me; I have no time
to ponder over that which
has been denied."**

~ Helen Keller

CHAPTER TWELVE

Acceptance is the Key-
How Gratitude Saved
My Life

By Monique Sayers

I can still remember that day of my near-death experience vividly; it was my 36th birthday and I had paddled out to my favorite surf break inadeptly called "Impossibles." In my world, nothing had ever seemed impossible, as I am a firm believer in possibility. I had lived my dream life in Bali for almost two years where my days were filled with surfing, teaching students and enjoying island life. As I breathe in, I can still smell the salt in my hair, feel the warm ocean permeate my skin and see the tropical fish deep below my surfboard as I waited for the next set of oncoming waves. Surfing for me had always been a place of *gratitude* and connection with nature as I watched the waving palm trees that divinely reached into the heavens on the distant shore. *Appreciation* has been something I have practiced sincerely — well, except for the times I rejected it like a lonely child crying for more love.

The moment before a wave appears, it's like connecting with the gods. There's trust, excitement and surrender, knowing the ocean ultimately is the divine leader in what it serves; no two waves are ever the same. As I stared at the tranquil movement of water starting to bulge as a set arrived, I felt connected and ready to paddle. I paddled left hard and danced the waves to meet the white foam on the shallow, sharp shore. Elated, I stood on the jagged toothed reef with my surf boots donned and a dimpled smile on my face. What an amazing birthday I had planned: breakfast with my husband, a midday surf and divine dinner to follow. Little did I know, another major gift was about to arrive.

It all happened so quickly; one moment I was on a luminous wave, the next I was in a pool of stark blood. As I stood on the colorful coral after my ride, the surf thundering its foam onto the reef fiercely. I pulled my leg rope back towards me, but my board had other plans. It bounced on the reef and was thrown up into the sky. As I looked up into the warm sun, my board fell in slow motion towards my head. BANG. BUMP. THUMP. Like a frozen statue, I stood as its glorious glass pointed nose hit my face, piercing my skin like a severe gunshot. Another surfer — the only other surfer — paddled straight over to my rescue. Her name was Katherine. She too, was a local expat surfer. I still remember the look on her face as she glared at the ocean of scarlet blood flooding down my face all over my body. I asked her if she could help me get home and she replied, "We're going straight to the hospital." At this point, I knew it was serious and that the only way to manage it was to be *grateful.*

The shock had taken over my body in the best way possible. I felt highly alert, calm and extremely present like a lion chasing prey. A lion doesn't cry; it focuses and stays quiet before it leaps on its victory. I didn't move into my pain body; instead, I was focused on survival. I knew the only way to get through this was two things: number one, do not look in the mirror or I may faint at sight. Number two, be *highly grateful* for absolutely everything, as negativity could worsen my situation. My instinct knew that *gratitude* was going to be my savior. As Katherine led me up the rock wall stairs of the "Impossibles" surf break, I humbly expressed how *grateful* I was to have her support. She mirrored back my gratitude and started to play along with me. Her words touched me deeply, "Wow, we are so lucky that I have a car here ready to drive you to Bali's best hospital."

The truth was, I was feeling so damn *grateful* for Katherine's presence. If she had not been there, then who else could have saved me? Life is not about, "what if" scenarios. Nothing is a coincidence. As we traveled together to Nusa Dua Hospital, I shared that she was a living angel. She glanced at me whimsically and shared that this was not her first time being a rescuer. Her fiancé had died in her arms in another freak accident. I feel this experience we both had was literally coming from the heavens, a cathartic process for us both. We arrived at the icy hospital as shock started to cool my body, especially as I was only wearing a wet bikini, surf boots and Katherine's sarong.

I was in such a high state of *gratitude* as the emergency staff came to attend to me. Katherine had left to bring me clothes and to inform my husband. How did I keep in such a state of *gratitude* while literally being in survival mode? Easy. I had practiced the art of "being *grateful* anyway," for many years. *Gratitude* is a feeling. It's not simply words. It's a feeling inside of me that I tap into, a sense of love and peace. Whenever I needed to quickly access the feeling, I would close my eyes and feel my breath going in and out. A sense of peace would create the feeling of *gratitude*. At the hospital, I did not dare close my eyes. I needed to be fully present. I could still access *gratitude* through my breath with my eyes open. The doctor explained that my maxilla (cheekbone) was broken and I would need a metal plate inside to replace my bone. I would need plastic surgery on my face, and I was lucky the board hadn't gone any closer to my brain. At this moment, I felt so *grateful* just for being alive but I still needed to make it through the surgery. I laid down and allowed the anesthetic to take over and trust that I would wake again.

As I woke up hazily, I realized, "Wow, I'm still here. I am still alive." I had made it through the surgery! As my eyes opened, I saw my concerned husband, who had been asleep in the hospital armchair. He jumped up and embraced me. He pulled a face which he quickly hid, so I knew my face must be nasty. I remember asking him for water, but the voice that came from me was not my usual sweet sound, but more like a ghastly monster. What had happened to my voice? My husband had tears when he heard my voice. I still had faith that everything was going to work out fine and I would speak normally again. As he held up the mirror for me to see, I was greeted by the Joker. My whole right cheek was covered in stitches from nose to jawline. I can still feel the deep-rooted pain, the taste of metallic blood and numbness that intoxicated my whole being. It was horrific to witness, especially through my vain eyes. I have always been blessed with good health, a good body and good looks — then this accident had come into my life to shake things up. The lesson was about self-love and loving myself anyway, despite my new ugly face. Now, this was where the real learning about *gratitude* took place.

The next months all blended into one with deep healing of the body and mind. I left my Bali island dream behind and flew back to Australia for simple pleasures like a warm shower with clean water. Katherine had promised to see me again when I would next return to the island. This moment felt like a turning point. "Yes, I am alive. Yes, I am lucky, but I want my old life back," were my repeated thoughts. In Bali, I had it all! I had my absolute dream job of teaching children at an international school and it broke my heart that I wouldn't be teaching them, but instead I'd be healing. I had my island days of pure pleasure, whether it was playing under a waterfall, praying at a temple or surfing my favorite break, which I wouldn't be doing anymore. The party was now over.

So, how exactly did I heal and stay in the state of *gratitude* at a time when I felt frustrated lying in bed, tired and wanting to turn back time? *Gratitude* is like a two-sided coin. One side is straightforward to manage. It's the side where I would feel *grateful* and happy. There is nothing really to do but to stay in a positive vibe. The other side of the coin is where I would feel *ungrateful* and not positively view the world. Whenever a coin is flipped, it can land on either face, and this is the game of life. Sometimes there were highs and sometimes there were lows until I discovered the third side. It's a third dimensional aspect of a vibrant coin that is not seen visually. For me, this is a feeling of acceptance. To accept everything as it is, whether it is high or low and to be able to feel at peace with both. This is the ultimate state of *gratitude*.

When I was healing from my accident in Australia, I used the principle of acceptance a lot to be able to create peace and *gratitude* in my life. Whenever I looked in the mirror at the new version of me, I could choose to see a beauty that became a beast or a beast that was becoming a beauty — just like the two-sided coin. Both were not helpful. If I kept focusing on the loss of my beauty, it would not help and if I were to keep wishing for my face to change, it would cause pain. So, I would practice *gratitude* for what was real. Whatever I would feel, I would allow. If pain was there, I welcomed it. If happiness was there, I received it.

To get into this state of *gratitude*, I would go into a form of meditation. With my eyes closed, I would simply breathe. I would allow my mind to wander or feel peace or whatever it was feeling without controlling it. I would breathe deeply and be a witness to what was there. Then, as I would open my eyes, I would say, "Thank you. Thank you for feeling ugly," or "Thank you for feeling happy," and the same for whatever feeling was present. I wouldn't try to change what was already real for me at that moment. It worked every time because there was no tricking the mind. It would bring peace to whatever emotion was being experienced.

As I lay in bed, healing my painful face for what felt like endless weeks at my mum's home in Australia, I reflected on my life and just how far I had come. Before living in Bali, I had lived in Sydney for seven years. After graduating as a teacher, I decided to work in a corporate role as a software trainer on big, fancy projects. I was a single woman in the city on a mission: to be happy and in love with a prince. When this fantasy did not playout, I would feel even more lonely and a deep-rooted pain would engulf my body. I would feel **ungrateful** during this period of my life, which only attracted more of the same bitter energy.

If you had asked me at this time, "Are you grateful?" I would have answered, "Yes," until I realized the truth was actually "No." I had it all — an amazing job flying around Australia to deliver training to ASX Top 100 companies. I was voted "Trainer of the Year," by Bondi Surf Lifesaving Club and I completed a marathon. My weekends were filled with pleasure, parties and fun in the sun. Whatever I wanted I could get it — all except for one thing: I didn't have love. Ultimately, this was self-love and actualization. I would sit and write gratitude lists, yet the power of my mind was stronger than my ability to envision beyond my pain. This is no longer my reality, but at that time, my *gratitude* list was like this:

1. I'm grateful for surfing (but I don't have love).

2. I'm grateful for my family (I'm jealous my sister has love and I don't).

3. I'm grateful for my job (but my heart feels closed).

It seemed like the more I tried to solve my problem of feeling stuck, not in love and confused, the more it felt like more problems would appear. I turned more towards meditation, which I had thought would be an easy band-aid method to be able to use the power of attraction to somehow trick myself into receiving my magical prince. What I want to say is that, "yes, the power of attraction actually does work, but it also brings all the things that don't work to the surface to be changed within." The more meditation I experienced, the more I felt like I had lost who I was, my identity and my ability to have "fake feelings," no matter what. The rapture of *ingratitude* was at its most potent, so much so, that I decided to take radical action.

Walking into our high-rise office with spectacular views of the city, despite all I had been given, I knew I had to leave. I felt like I could not go on stuck in a lie. I asked for time off and I flew to India with one goal: to become free from all suffering. I can still smell the incense and the energy of seers awakened to higher realms, the colorful robes of people calling me into their bazaars or offering to be my tour guide. I felt completely safe amongst the crowds of millions as I headed towards the Oneness Temple in Chennai, which is an awakening powerhouse. This temple is a sacred place where people from all over the world come from any race, religion or culture and take a profound spiritual awakening course with the enlightened Avatars, Sri Amma and Sri Bhagavan. The moment I sat in their divine presence on the first Darshan, tears of pure *gratitude* flooded my entire essence. I experienced, for the first time, exactly what *appreciation* is. *Gratitude* is not a list. It's not something in the mind. It's not something that you say but don't mean. *Gratitude* is a deeply connected feeling from the heart center that radiates as the essence of full presence and peace with everything on Earth.

Many deep teachings have become truths within my energy center at this mystical temple. What I learned about *gratitude* is how to practice acceptance. Sri Amma Bhagavan shared a mantra, "To see is to be free," which we contemplated daily. This is something to contemplate deeply. It starts by being able to see yourself, then being able to accept what you see. It could be a pleasurable or painful experience but staying present to it will ultimately set you free. As it deepens, there's a paradox, as there is nothing or nobody to see. I still use this one mantra every day and it always brings me back to either a place of *gratitude* or *ingratitude* and acceptance of both states of consciousness. If I am *grateful* for one thing but ungrateful for another, I realize I am in conflict inside. Deep meditation has changed my brain's neurocircuits to be able to feel at peace in any state. This is how I faced my surfing incident so quickly, as I had been practicing it for years.

At the luminous temple, we meditators completed processes regarding how *ungrateful* we were to our parents, which mirrored all other relationships in our lives. I remember reflecting on my parents and how I had blamed them for different reasons. Within the process, I was shown to be grateful to them for all they have done for me and that they, too, were once innocent children. I witnessed my parents as children and from this place, I was flooded with tears. I am forever *grateful* to my parents for bringing me into this world. I'm also deeply thankful to Sri Amma Bhagavan for awakening my being to divine consciousness.

After completing my training in India, I decided to move to Bali permanently to teach children and simply be "me." With my new awakened energy, everything fell into place. Instead of feeling confused, I felt certain. Instead of feeling lonely, I felt whole. Instead of feeling unloved, I felt love for everyone and everything. It was such a defining moment in my consciousness on this Earth and I knew it was time to go forth on my mission. I manifested a beautiful place to live by the beach in Uluwatu, where I met my husband, Martin, so magically and easily after a day of surfing. I was living pure happiness and *gratitude* for life itself.

After a year and a half together in Bali, I remember smiling radiantly at my husband as I sipped a hot chocolate, excited for the birthday surf to follow. He decided to snap a photo of my happy, cute dimpled smile at the local Balinese café owned by one of my students. Little did I know that this would be the last photo of my dimpled face before I gathered my board ready to surf. You just never know what's next in life, only each moment. As I looked in the mirror in Australia, I was greeted by a long, tender scar on my right cheek. While my beautiful dimple was gone forever, the scar was a reminder that nothing in life is permanent. I felt so *grateful* for being alive and truly lucky for the recovery I had created for myself. I had spent hours a day in the space of self-love, which included daily meditation, connecting with nature and feeling gratitude for life. My voice was now normal, the muscles in my cheek were getting stronger and I could even smile without it hurting anymore. I had the gift of life!

With a smile as big as the vast ocean, I returned to Bali after three months of deep healing in Australia. Life felt so good! As I entered the classroom, my students ran up and hugged me with *gratitude*. As I felt the wind in my hair on my scooter, I felt so *grateful*. As I dove into the glassy, tropical ocean, I melted weightlessly into her loving waves. The accident now made sense to me. There is no such thing as an accident, only a series of incidents and what is learned in each moment from them. *Gratitude* is a reflection of you. Whether you're *grateful* or not, the key is to accept yourself with scars and all. Breathe deeply and contemplate, "To see is to be free," as guided by Sri Amma Bhagavan. May this story serve you and may every single word bring forth even more divine peace and *gratitude* in your precious life.

"I don't have to chase extraordinary moments to find happiness. It's right in front of me if I'm paying attention and practicing gratitude."

~ Brene Brown

AUTHOR BIOGRAPHIES

John Spender

CHAPTER ONE

John Spender is a 23-time international best-selling co-author, who didn't learn how to read and write at a basic level until he was ten years old. He has since traveled the world and started many businesses, leading him to create the best-selling book series A Journey of Riches. He is an award-winning international speaker and movie maker.

John worked as an international NLP trainer and has coached thousands of people from various backgrounds through all sorts of challenges. From the borderline homeless to very wealthy individuals, he has helped many people get in touch with their truth to create a life on their terms.

John's search for answers to living a fulfilling life has taken him to work with Native American Indians in the Hills of San Diego, the forests of Madagascar, swimming with humpback whales in

Tonga, exploring the Okavango Delta of Botswana and the Great Wall of China. He's traveled from Chile to Slovakia, Hungary to the Solomon Islands, the mountains of Italy to the streets of Mexico.

Everywhere his journey has taken him, John has discovered a hunger among people to find a new way to live, with a yearning for freedom of expression. His belief is that everyone has a book in them was born.

He is now a writing coach, having worked with more than 200 authors from 40 different countries for the A Journey of Riches series (http://ajourneyofriches.com/) and his publishing house, Motion Media International, has published 20 non-fiction titles to date.

John also co-wrote and produced the movie documentary Adversity, starring Jack Canfield, Rev. Micheal Bernard Beckwith, Dr. John Demartini and many more, coming soon in 2020. Moreover, you can bet there will be a best-selling book to follow!

Julie Blouin

CHAPTER TWO

J ulie Blouin lives in Cornwall, Ontario, Canada, a small city located on the Saint Lawrence River on the border of the United States. Julie loves traveling and she speaks English, French and intermediate Spanish.

She is an author, a mindset coach, and a motivational speaker who uses her own struggles and challenges to inspire and motivate others to become the best version of themselves. She graduated from the University of Ottawa in 1999 with a Bachelor of Social Sciences, and she is also a Certified Professional Coach from Fowler International Academy of Professional Coaching.

Julie helps her clients focus on personal growth and success by helping them increase their dose of self-love, self-confidence, self-worth, self-care, self-discipline and overcome self-limiting beliefs to thrive in the areas of: career, relationships, wealth, health, spirituality, and well-being. She enriches the lives of her clients by identifying blind spots, developing a clear vision, and by helping them to take action to achieve their full potential, reach their goals, and ultimately live their best life.

Website: www.julieblouin.com For inquiries:
info@julieblouin.com

Kylie & Rusty

CHAPTER THREE

R usty is a cheeky chestnut Standardbred horse, bred as a pacer in harness racing. However, he apparently came last in both his races, and so he moved on to be a riding horse. Kylie and Shane found him some months later with a lovely family in the country, and this is where their journey together began.

As time progresses, Rusty grows in confidence and strength.

His curious and loyal personality shines through, and the difference people see in him today is incredible.

Rusty's complete transformation over the last few years has been nothing short of remarkable.

As for Kylie, growing up in the country meant she was lucky enough to have horses from a fairly young age.

However, when she moved to the city for university, she put her work and study first, and she struggled with keeping a healthy work/life balance for years. She was working as a life coach in leadership, wellness, and performance, when she finally decided she needed a hobby other than work, physical exercise or study.

It was then that she came up with the grand idea of getting a horse, and to be honest, life has not been the same since.

This is their story, *"Moments of Reflection in Gratitude."*

Instagram: somethingrustyred

Simone Wadell

CHAPTER FOUR

S imone Waddell is an award-winning singer, songwriter, voice coach, Certified Life Coach, workshop, and retreat designer and facilitator, speaker, and writer. Through her *You Have A Voice* events and programs, she has become an inspiring mentor and role model. Simone will help you *Find Your Voice, Empower Your Soul, and Live the Song of Your Life.*

Simone has performed professionally in China, Japan, the U.S.A, Norway, and her homeland, Australia. She was the first Australian to receive a scholarship to Berklee, one of the top music schools in the world. Simone has released four albums, two EPs, and multiple singles. Her original music videos have over half a million views worldwide online.

As well as her Bachelor of Arts Degree in Contemporary Music, Simone completed her Research Masters Degree in Jazz Vocals on a scholarship at the Sydney Conservatorium of Music, with a High Distinction.

Career highlights: touring with the Grammy-nominated artist, Taylor Dayne, numerous performances for national leaders at Parliament House, and performing for Australian Music Week as the opening act for the jazz icon Vince Jones.

Her recent work in Uganda coaching the Watoto Children's Choir and the Teenage Worship Academy was a treasured time in her life.

Through some tough life lessons dealing with domestic violence, and overcoming false beliefs regarding staying in abusive situations, Simone rebuilt her life from the ground up. She ultimately evolved, through the power of God, music, and the unconditional love of friends and family, to have more awareness of how to change her destiny and live the *song of her life.*

Simone would love to have you stay in touch.
Please contact her via her website www.simonewaddell.com
Email info@simonewaddell.com
Facebook: Simone Waddell

King Gabriel

CHAPTER FIVE

K ing Gabriel is a world-renowned Spiritual Explorer, Healing Practitioner, award-winning author, and Spiritual Teacher.

Referred to by some as the Spiritual Life Engineer, He has the unified goal of allowing Everyone to recognize, realize and experience the fact that They are free to create and live the beautiful lives that They may have imagined, but have seen as difficult or unattainable up to this point.

He remembers being One with The Source of Being before beginning this part of the experience, and He has the memory of this feeling and the qualitative content of the communion.

His achievements include: Spiritual Practitioner/Teacher, Certified Reiki Master, Qi Gong Practitioner, Electrical Engineer (BS), Musician, Published Author, former Professional Athlete and Coach in multiple sports; has directly assisted thousands of clients in Individual meetings, spoken in front of masses as large as 26 million participants, and has shared the stage with many great Spiritual Leaders, highly regarded Speakers, Mystics and

Musicians including Rev. Michael Bernard Beckwith, John Gray, Lisa Nichols, Chaka Khan, The Black Eyed Peas, Stevie Wonder, and many Others. He has also directly trained a Head Coach for the Los Angeles Defense Department for over eight years with great success.

He has created, utilized, and shared many simple and effective tools and practices that have shifted the minds of Participants in ways that are beyond belief for Some.

The consistency of His efforts is seen in the wonderful and consistent results that have been attained by Those with whom He has worked.

His favorite quote is "I Love," (by Himself), and it is a declaration that the Who, what, where, and how usually attached to the idea of Loving is insignificant. The expression of this state of being, however, is a powerful vibration and an acceptance of the ability to choose Love in all its beautiful paths of expression, without a validation or readily apparent reason.

Contact:
Facebook: King Gabriel QuincyCollymore or
www.facebook.com/kgqcollymore

email:
kinggabrielinfo@gmail.com

Group Page:
Page with King Gabriel and Tara Antler, His Wife and Business Partner
www.facebook.com/groups/iriseandthrive/?ref=share

Elizabeth Ross-Boag

CHAPTER SIX

Elizabeth is a follower of the Gaudiya Sampradaya spiritual lineage. In 1999, she was initiated by her Spiritual Teacher Srila Govinda Maharaj and received personal instruction in Bhakti Yoga. Since receiving his guidance and encouragement, Elizabeth earned a Double Degree-The Bachelor of Education and Bachelor of Human Movement/Exercise Science while concurrently raising four beautiful children and pursuing yoga training, including extensive travel to India, Indonesia, and Timor Leste.

Elizabeth is also the founder of 'Eastern Lifestyles' and has spent the last five years motivating individuals and communities to take steps towards a sustainable future, inspiring eco-friendly initiatives in food production, building design, community economics, and community development.

Elizabeth is conversant in the life balance of optimal health and is dedicated to helping others discover the natural way to a healthy and happy lifestyle.

For more information: www.easternlifestyles.com

Patrick Oei

CHAPTER SEVEN

P rincipal Consultant, Paragon Dynamics, a versatile
Trainer/Consultant who has trained & lectured at many
companies/ Institutions of Higher Learning and also
personally coached many CEOs, Directors, Managers & Execs.

He is equipped in Civil Engineering, Admin Management,
Organization & Methods, Sales & Marketing, Management
Consultancy and Marketing Management, Plus High Honors in an
MBA in International Finance and Marketing. He also has
qualifications in Training & Development and American
Management Association (AMA) & also ACTA certified. He also
holds a CEHA.

As a Master Clinical Hypnotherapist, he has conducted & helped
many in Mindfulness, Stress Reduction, and other issues.

As a Belbin Accredited Facilitator, he has helped teams work
better in a work or common-team environment.

He has worked in Engineering, Plant Management, Building
Development, Special Projects, and Sales and Marketing, setting

up a Japanese Local Joint Venture from scratch and becoming its 1st COO.

He is the first in SE Asia to earn the Distinguished Toastmaster DTM award twice and has served in various leadership positions from President to the highest level as its highest-ranking Officer as the District Governor now known as District Director.

He was elected to the International Board of Directors in 2014 and just completed his two year term.

1st three persons to be awarded the Crystal Award by the then-National-Productivity Board, Patrick has conducted various Programs from Change Management, Presentation Skills, Team Building, Leadership, Personal Empowerment & Transformation, Mindfulness, Diversity for numerous companies over the last 30 years.

Patrick has been featured on 90.5FM, 93.8FM Mediacorp, Capital TV in Malaysia and also Berita Satu TV in Indonesia,

Patrick may be contacted at +6594319443 and at ParagonDynamics@gmail.com

Jacinta Legg

CHAPTER EIGHT

J acinta Legg is in her early thirties. She is a mother of a two children under the age of four. Motherhood for her has been challenging of course but the most rewarding experience she has had yet. She is a strong, open-minded woman who believes life is what you make of it. She has a firm belief in living a happy life and learning from her challenges and experiences. She loves a good opportunity and loves to find time for her passion hobbies.

She has not had your normal textbook education and study. She has handcrafted her career through her own visions, education, and hands-on work experience. She found her wings through experiences, challenges, and learning the ability to overcome them.

Before she reached her twenties, she had owned a house with no deposit, she had a fashion modelling contract at seventeen, and was involved in the Lilly Team raising money for The Royal Children's hospital appeal, which led to an opportunity to be an entrant in Miss Universe. She then travelled and built her career on these solid bases.

She always had a genuine interest in business and how it is that businesses become successful and make their profits. This has led to naturally forming a career and study based around Marketing and the Advertising Industry for the last ten years.

Through just doing what she believed in, she has found her own gratitude in her journey and appreciates the hard work she has put in to get where she is today. Her focus is now primarily on her family and working towards growing within her industry and becoming a marketing expert. Maybe one day she quotes "I may even capitalize on my own business or inventive ideas."

Jacinta Legg
Instagram @jacintalee123

Tina Louise Vercillo

CHAPTER NINE

T ina Louise Vercillo is a cancer survivor. She has spent the better part of five years refining her attitude of gratitude by overcoming a myriad of challenges in her life.

Tina works as a software systems Trainer and Documentation Specialist at a reputable Australian University. Her passion lies in coaching, a craft she has been called to share through assisting clients in creating a life of wellness and limitless possibilities.

Bordering on Woo Woo, Tina finds the perfect balance of conventional daily practices alongside alternative healing therapies, uses an array of therapeutic grade essential oils, and practices daily meditations, all while living her best life.

Tina is the President of the board of a not-for-profit organization. She believes that change occurs when a group of like-minded individuals comes together to advocate for a better world. As a volunteer, she is passionate about creating change in her local community with the hope to branch out nationally.

Being a mother is one of Tina's greatest achievements. She hopes that by witnessing her life's triumphs, her daughter will continue to become more resilient and empowered.

As she redefines herself, Tina enthusiastically embraces the lessons that each day brings and finds, no matter how small, a piece of gratitude in it all.

Most days, you will find Tina sitting peacefully in the garden, listening to one of Dr. Joe Dispenza's meditations, with her sweet scent of Patchouli and Ylang Ylang essential oils in the air, practicing the art of living.

To get in touch with Tina:

www.facebook.com/tina.louise.wellnesscoach

tinalouiselc@icloud.com

Joanne Singleton

CHAPTER TEN

Born and raised in Vancouver, British Columbia, Canada, Joanne has had a career over the past 35 years that has engaged her in both the legal and real estate industries, locally and worldwide.

Although the legal field and real estate professions have been the core focus of Joanne's career, she has always had a boundless vocation for writing, which has persisted throughout her countless personal and professional endeavors.

Joanne is an Amazon Best-Selling Author for her book, *Daughter of Kate,* and she has written the screenplay for *Daughter of Kate,* for which it was originally intended.

A Journey of Riches, The Attitude of Gratitude is Joanne's second published accomplishment, with this being a true honor and privilege to have been invited to be a part of. Joanne's creative pathway will continue to light her way and gratefully share with all. Please visit Joanne's website at www.joannesingleton.com.

Joanne cherishes her family time, loves to travel, meeting new people from all walks of life, and sharing a fine meal with those she loves. My children… this is for you.

"Try not to let life get in the way of what's important."

Anup Batra

CHAPTER ELEVEN

Anup Batra is a tech entrepreneur, a spiritual soul, and a mentor to businesses owners who fuse profit with purpose. He was born and brought up in India by highly educated and accomplished parents. The culture of the family was around generosity, discipline and achievements.

His father was an Engineer with the Government and got transferred to a different city every three years. In the time it would take to make new friends and settle in school and the new city, it would be time to pack the bags and move. The early childhood life was exciting and provided for new experiences, but it also brought with it instability and lack of continuity.

His father was immensely respected, generous, and loving. Having himself risen to the highest ranks and acclaimed for his work, he had very high standards both for himself and Anup.

Anup grew up to be a Marine Engineer and sailed around the world experiencing the most exciting life, including severe storms, pirates attack, and glittery nightlife.

In a chance event, his ship came to Australia where he fell in love with the people. He found Australians to be very warm, social, and enterprising.

When his ship left Australia, Anup made up his mind to return later.

He went on to do an MBA program, after which he joined a Management Consultancy.

While the work was enjoyable, the corporate culture did not inspire Anup.

Around that time, an opportunity presented itself and the Universe manifested his Australian dream.. He has been living in Melbourne, Australia for the last sixteen years.

He launched a digital marketing business in Australia two years after arriving in Melbourne, and within one year, the business was embraced and recognized by business leaders as a distinctive agency.

Through the years, Anup has developed a passion for spirituality and celebrates the gift of love and gratitude as two vital forces in his life.

He has a knack for turning crisis into opportunity and is helping Australians to bring out their creativity to overcome adversity, flourish, and prosper.

Anup loves to meet new people and make friends. He would love to hear from you. Connect with him on Facebook or drop a line.

Monique Sayers

CHAPTER TWELVE

Monique Sayers is an Australian born teacher, writer, lover of life, mama, and entrepreneur. Living most of her life abroad, she considers herself a citizen of the world who values peace, service, and authenticity. Whether she's been teaching children in Bali, trekking Nepal, walking with lions in Kenya, surfing the Maldives, or running a marathon in Sydney, Monique is all about living life to the fullest.

Having taught almost 20,000 students from all over the world, Monique is passionate about her offering. Her gift is that she teaches with joy, connection, and intuition, making every class unique to that student's needs. She learns from every student just as much as she teaches them. Her guidance has always come from Gandhi's stance to "be the change you wish to see in the world."

Monique is the first to admit she's not perfect. She spent many years in search of more joy in life. This led her to a trip to India, where she was gifted awakening at the Oneness Temple. Her life changed forever. Not only did she receive profound peace but also the ability to share this energetic transmission with others as a blessing giver.

Monique dedicates her chapter to Coral (her daughter) and to anyone who is calling more gratitude into their life. May every page bless you and guide you on your journey. If you'd like to connect with Monique, write to inspiration@moniquecoral.com and she will send you a PDF gift of gratitude tips.

"When gratitude becomes your default setting, life changes."

~ Nancy Leigh Demoss

AFTERWORD

I hope you enjoyed the collection of heartfelt stories, wisdom and vulnerability shared. Storytelling is the oldest form of communication, and I hope you feel inspired to take a step toward living a fulfilling life. Feel free to contact any of the authors in this book, or the other books in this series.

The proceeds of this book will go to feeding many of the rural Balinese families that are struggling through the current pandemic.

Other books in the series are…

Facing your Fears : A Journey of Riches, Book Twenty Two

Returning to Love : A Journey of Riches, Book Twenty One
https://www.amazon.com/dp/B08C54M2RB

Develop Inner Strength : A Journey of Riches, Book Twenty
https://www.amazon.com/dp/1925919153

Building your Dreams : A Journey of Riches, Book Nineteen
https://www.amazon.com/dp/B081KZCN5R

Liberate your Struggles : A Journey of Riches, Book Eighteen
https://www.amazon.com/dp/1925919099

In Search of Happiness : A Journey of Riches, Book Seventeen
https://www.amazon.com/dp/B07R8HMP3K

Tapping into Courage : A Journey of Riches, Book Sixteen
https://www.amazon.com/dp/B07NDCY1KY

The Power Healing : A Journey of Riches, Book Fifteen
https://www.amazon.com/dp/B07LGRJQ2S

The Way of the Entrepreneur: A Journey Of Riches, Book Fourteen
https://www.amazon.com/dp/B07KNHYR8V

Discovering Love and Gratitude: A Journey Of Riches, Book Thirteen
https://www.amazon.com/dp/B07H23Q6D1

Transformational Change: A Journey Of Riches, Book Twelve
https://www.amazon.com/dp/B07FYHMQRS

Finding Inspiration: A Journey Of Riches, Book Eleven
https://www.amazon.com/dp/B07F1LS1ZW

Building your Life from Rock Bottom: A Journey Of Riches, Book Ten
https://www.amazon.com/dp/B07CZK155Z

Transformation Calling: A Journey Of Riches, Book Nine
https://www.amazon.com/dp/B07BWQY9FB

Letting Go and *Embracing* the New: A *Journey Of* Riches, *Book* Eight
https://www.amazon.com/dp/B079ZKT2C2

Making Empowering Choices: A Journey Of Riches, Book Seven
https://www.amazon.com/Making-Empowering-Choices-Journey-Riches-ebook/dp/B078JXMK5V

The Benefit of Challenge: A Journey Of Riches, Book Six
https://www.amazon.com/dp/B0778S2VBD

Personal Changes: A Journey Of Riches, Book Five
https://www.amazon.com/dp/B075WCQM4N

Dealing with Changes in Life: A Journey Of Riches, Book Four
https://www.amazon.com/dp/B0716RDKK7

Afterword

Making Changes: A Journey Of Riches, Book Three
https://www.amazon.com/dp/B01MYWNI5A

The Gift In Challenge: A Journey Of Riches, Book Two
https://www.amazon.com/dp/B01GBEML4G

From Darkness into the Light: A Journey Of Riches, Book One
https://www.amazon.com/dp/B018QMPHJW

Thank you to all the authors that have shared aspects of their lives in the hope that it will inspire others to live a bigger version of themselves. I heard a great saying from Jim Rohan, "You can't complain and feel grateful at the same time." At any given moment, we have a choice to either feel like a victim of life, or be connected and grateful for it. I hope this book helps you to feel grateful, and go after your dreams. For more information about contributing to the series, visit http://ajourneyofriches.com/ . Furthermore, if you enjoyed reading this book, we would appreciate your review on Amazon to help getour message out to more readers.

Manufactured by Amazon.ca
Bolton, ON

15854841R00120